The Birth of Something Beautiful

The Story of Tushikamane

This book is dedicated to those
impoverished, ill-educated,
rural women of poor countries,
whose insight and determination
could have such a positive impact on our world.

It is also dedicated to charities such as
'Mission Morogoro' and
'Women and Children First',
whose wonderful and selfless work gives,
to those who have never had them,
hope,
opportunity …
and a voice.

The beginning

Yesterday, I saved three lives in rural Tanzania. The previous Friday, I planted out my hollyhock and lupin seedlings in the front garden, before going for three pints in The Oak. In a couple of months, I will be back in The Oak relishing those pints, those friends, that familiar life, and feeling, for a while, the inappropriateness of my 21st century English values and preferences.

Or perhaps not? Perhaps I will be changed? If I have the skills to make a difference to the desperate natural mortality in this beautiful country, will I want to stay? Don't worry, my lovely wife and family, I will return on time, thinner, browner, wiser and more full of peanuts than any Englishman since Albert Schweitzer (who was neither English nor full of peanuts, but when you start a simile, you have to finish it, and I hope you inferred that the culinary choices in rural Tanzania, in a house with two men unused to wielding a skillet, are limited in the extreme, and are largely influenced by knowing which foods can be bought locally that contain neither goat gristle nor salmonella.)

My journey began a week ago on the comfortable evening flight from Birmingham to Dar es Salaam via Dubai. Well, actually, my journey began 30 years ago when I did my first Caesarean section in Africa. I had been a surgeon, peremptorily removing at will unwanted parts of people. It took me a few years to realise it, but from the moment that my hand miraculously pulled a living, crying, beautiful, wriggling baby from a mother, I was an obstetrician.

Thirty years on, I am retired from my job as lead obstetrician in Coventry, and am back in Africa, to see if I can make a difference in just a short two-month visit.

A difference is sorely needed. Around half a million women each year give birth in Tanzania and, every two hours, one of them dies. In England, it would be one death every week. Of the survivors, far too many are left with the crippling disability of fistula (urine constantly emptying through the vagina because of a hole in the bladder), and so many lose their baby that it is hardly even a matter for consolation. The causes are deeply rooted, and I cower at the prospect of trying to influence any. I will not, for instance, be able to stop the rain in summer. If lakes have not yet realised that the hot sun is just tricking them into becoming clouds, then I doubt that I can persuade them otherwise. No wonder the water is angry when it fills the river beds, turns the roads to mud and prevents the passage of anything but hippo triathletes.

Neither can I change the beliefs of women in distant dusty villages, nor the practices of the traditional birth attendants, whose tea explodes your surprised uterus into action before you – or your baby – even has a chance to draw breath. On Thursday, a woman came in from a remote place, with a dead baby and a ruptured uterus. Her other three labours had been normal, but the birth attendant underestimated the power of this practised womb. In the rainy season, the woman would have been another two-hour statistic, and I would have felt the futility of my good intentions.

But they are not futile, as the three lives testify! At 5.30 yesterday morning, in inky blackness, the security guard rattled the mosquito screens on the windows of our old colonial bungalow. He explained in Swahili the need for me to come, and I followed (in English). A sad, dimly-lit room in one corner of the hospital quadrangle is the labour ward. A tiny 18-year-old had arrived, and had been in labour for far too long. The baby's head was stuck in the wrong position, wedged deep, deep, deep in the vagina. Someone, surprisingly, had listened to the fetal heart rate (what difference would it make?), and it was wearily slow. Last week, a Caesarean section would have been ordered. The theatre night-staff would have been called from their homes in the village. The generator would have been powered up and the feeble yellow lights would have reluctantly awoken. Habel, an excellent technician trained in anaesthesia, would have checked the drawers to see whether any spinal anaesthesia was available and, discovering none, would have poured the halothane into the gas machine.

The frightened girl would have been lying on a rubber sheet in the corridor, without the luxury of anyone to comfort her. Eventually, the Assistant Medical Officer's expert hand, reaching far down into her pelvis, would have discovered the degree to which the baby's head was wedged into the friable and swollen tissues. Whatever it took to get the dead baby out would have been done, during which the mother's weak condition would have been furthered compromised by blood loss and the inevitable entry of bacteria. A few days later after failing to stop the post-partum haemorrhage, she perhaps would have left these worries behind her.

4

But that is not what happened. Five minutes after I arrived, I was holding a desperately hypoxic baby in my arms, thanks to the wonders of the hand-held Kiwi vacuum delivery tool. (Thanks Nicholas and Pelican Healthcare! This baby lived because of your hard work and kindness in getting the Kiwis to me! Will Africa be able to afford these wonderful bits of kit?)

The baby was quickly wrapped in a kanga – a thin, brightly coloured all-purpose piece of material (well, all-purpose except for keeping a baby warm, as it turns out). When I called desperately for a dry one, the relatives unwrapped two more from the waists of passers-by. No neonatal crash team, no oxygen, no heating lamp, no suction, but half an hour of rubbing and pumping and squeezing and blowing and drying and warming, and a pink baby joined his confused mum, none of us really understanding what had just happened. Both are fine.

I skipped morning prayers and, eschewing the temptation of a quick peanut butter fix, slipped back home to celebrate with a special breakfast of fried cheese sandwich and a cup of tea. The tea was surprisingly good, despite being made of powdered tea, powdered milk and powdered rain-water.

I spent the morning lecturing the student nurses, having picked my way through the chickens scrimmaging around the nurses' home. It was the epicentre of culture clash. Imagine when you were at school, and instead of Miss Bunsen-Burner, the science teacher, in walks a Pacific Island chief in full feathered head-dress, who proceeds to teach you the history of Tahiti by beating the shrunken head of a former pupil on a goat's bladder stretched over a hollowed-out coconut. We have so much to learn to undo our cultural elitism, before we step into an African classroom.

In the afternoon, a Caesarean, but I was just the assistant so could not claim to have saved anything, except my need for sleep. The third life saved came later, and was more mundane. Another Caesarean, after nightfall. Another distressed baby. Another long wait. A general anaesthetic. This time, I am the surgeon, so as to show the afternoon's surgeon any differences in our technique. The baby came out easily, but was blue and seemingly lifeless, from a combination of oxygen starvation during labour, and general anaesthesia arriving via the mother. Leaving Dr Abdallah to sew up, I spent, for the second time that day, half an hour of vigour, pushing a baby up the steep slope towards

5

survival. Today I had the joy of seeing him getting to know the outside of his mum.

Berega hospital, Morogoro region, Tanzania

There is too much else to tell you this week – bats and termites; the wonderful Sion; showering with a cup; such friendly people; cleaning teeth with a torch in your mouth; Swahili faux pas; 100 things to do with a bean and more. And, of course, more on the answer to the question at the centre: can I help produce a sustainable difference?

Settling in

Eventually, Jim proved less of a problem than I had anticipated. Jim is the name of the bat who, embarrassingly for him, misinterpreted our absence of electricity at night as an invitation to the party. (To be honest, I cannot be certain that his name was Jim. To find out the first name of a bat is never easy and, in Jim's case, I suspect that he was deaf as well as blind.) He must have been more bewildered than annoyed to find just Sion and me; and in place of a winged arthrodpoda-fest, only beans and peanut butter. We made our apologies and slipped off to bed. A rattle of the bat flap, a moonlight flit, and Jim went out of our lives as quickly as he had come in.

In fact, given the number of Englishmen who have variously been mobbed, eaten, gored, mauled, chased, chewed on or sipped at by African fauna, I have had far less trouble than you might have imagined, for someone living six degrees below the Equator. For instance, in the eaves of the house lives a hornet (perhaps more than one – they are so difficult to tell apart) with a body the size of a sailor's forearm: but dive-bombing my Coke bottle is, to her, just friendly aerobatics. The monkeys that sometimes clamber playfully on the rooftop at sunset were mortified to hear me talk of an alarming screech. By day, butterflies flutter at half-speed. Scrawny chickens cluck, scrape, crow and peck at nothing in particular. Torpid dogs in the shade of a hard-baked house, raise a welcoming eyebrow. I haven't yet seen a mosquito (though two have seen me, and checked me out). African animals in mellow mode. As I walked to hospital the other evening along the dusty, broken, bumpy road of packed red clay, some Maasai drove towards me a small herd of deceptively wild-looking cattle.

They gently brushed by me as if I were a scratching post. One of them winked the wink he uses for a favoured heifer, but then snortingly suppressed a bovine chuckle. Good job because, short of side-stepping into a dry mud ditch or manfully grasping his worrying horns and wrestling him to the ground to demonstrate my complete un-heifer-ness, I had little option but to stand there and make rasping noises, as of bull on wood.

7

It is no little relief to know, then, that, at whatever time of day or night they call me from the hospital, I need not add fear of the unknown animal to fear of what awaits at the end of the six-minute stroll. What awaited me on Monday night was more shocking than anything I have seen, even in four years in Africa three eventful decades ago.

Shoulder dystocia means that the baby's head delivers, but then the shoulders are too broad to follow. It is one the most feared of childbirth complications by those who have the tee-shirt, because nature gives you just ten minutes from start to finish to see if you were paying attention on your obstetric emergencies course. The art of delivery, says the correct course is to rotate the baby to be face-down, by numerous means, at the same time as maximising the space by all but impossible flexion of the mother's knees and hips. Typically, shoulder dystocia happens in the UK when the baby is too big. Here, it happens more because the mother is too small. A lifetime of poverty and porridge leaves far too many women much tinier than their genes would have liked. For such women, a better result is to have an obstructed labour, as long as it happens where a Caesarean section can start them on the road to safer childbirth. Better that, than test the African response time to shoulder dystocia, and the Clinical Officer's memory of a distant and disembodied course.

NB – the following paragraph is seriously disturbing – you may want to skip it. But it is real life, and needs telling.

What the course does not tell you, however, is how to deal with shoulder dystocia when it began three days ago, when the six-stone woman, having had two Caesareans, was persuaded by relatives to stay in the village, to be delivered by the traditional birth attendant. It does not say how to persuade the same relatives the next day that, if the rest of the body of the long-dead baby has not yet been born, then help is needed. In particular, the course does not tell you how to console the inconsolable; how to de-terrify the terrifying; nor how to sit as the middle passenger on a motor-bike for a three-hour ride on fissured rocky roads, while between your legs is the head of your third baby, who died so long ago it that it seems like someone else's existence.

We had to sedate the mother to deliver the baby and, if there is a daily individual prayer allowance in heaven, then I used two weeks' worth in the next five minutes. Eventually, I managed to reach the posterior arm, and to slide it past the impacted body. Thereafter, the torque forces did their work and the limp, lifeless body tumbled out. An iodine-and-saline cleanse of the infected uterus, plus intravenous antibiotics, and the mum will this time survive. Dr Makanza, one of the excellent AMOs, was present and pushing supra-pubically, and I reflected on the irony of having a real-life demonstration as to how to manage this desperate condition.

Not that I have much to teach the AMOs, as it turns out, despite my putative purpose in being here to be a specialist mentor precisely to this grade of practitioner. In Tanzania, more than 80% of the population live in the rural parts of this vast, majestic and inaccessible land, but more than 80% of the doctors are in the cities. There are only 100 or so obstetricians in the entire country for a population nearly the size of England's. Complicated childbirth in the rural parts is thus served by Clinical Officers, who have completed a three-year course in how to deal with anything that arrives. After three more years working as a CO, it is possible to progress to AMO, by means of a further two years of full-time training. (The cost of the course for two years, including food and accommodation, is £2,000. Cheap? COs don't earn that in a year.) Two of our AMOs (Makanza and Abdallah), have done more Caesareans in their lives than most UK consultants, and certainly more emergency hysterectomies. What can I teach such people? Very sensibly, I have lowered my sights (or perhaps raised them), to ensuring that our student COs have picked clean my brain on how to deal with the crises in maternity that they are so certain to encounter.

And so it was in sombre mood that I picked my way back home that night, glad that the moon had finished the shady business that seems increasingly to occupy its time at nightfall. When the moon turns up late, whatever its excuses, the resulting utter blackness has something of a primeval creepiness to it. I say utter blackness, but of course my torch makes it less utter, powered as it is by good old Duracells. Reliable batteries here are as welcome as a simile. (You'll notice that I am still struggling a little with the second half of my comparisons. I would switch to metaphors if they weren't so brown.)

I am not sure how long the batteries will last, though. We rely on the torches to light everything after 6pm: our nocturnal bean-fest; our conversations; our annoying strumming of the guitar while the other person is trying to compose a text to his mum pretending that he doesn't want to break the guitar over your insensitive head, while you try to find that elusive Paul Simon chord that doesn't actually exist on the guitar; our teeth cleaning; our sluicing the torso with a cup or two of boiled river water; and our Kindle-ing ourselves to sleep at an absurdly premature hour. (The mission house does have solar panels, the most welcome gift of a past occupant, but with an archetypal African-ness, the power only seems to be available from the ageing batteries while the sun is actually shining. There is an electricity pylon 20 yards from the house, but as yet there is no way to find the monumental sum of £520 to connect up the house - much less the even larger sum needed to electrify the hospital properly. Sion had long since inured himself to a year of Duracell-powered evenings.)

Sion by the way (the Welsh version of the Irish 'Seán'), what can I say? What a wonderful 27-year-old human being. For a month, he has lived alone, immersed in a culture shock as profound as it is up-ending. And yet he remains humble, positive and determined to make a difference. An aside to you, Sion: sometimes the seeming senseless futility of situations might blind you to the immeasurably powerful effect of your loving kindness, extended freely. Simply being here, trying, caring and falteringly but surely progressing in Swahili, you are making more of a difference than any tangible result could ever quantify.

I seem to have reached my word limit and have hardly told you about the week. Of the sun and mountains; of the Monday market with its goods and chattels spread hopefully along the paths of the village; of the baby who died in my arms in theatre simply due to depressing delays; of visiting the hospital driver's three-hectare farm, as yet devoid of any intended flora or fauna, which he is slowly buying for £48; of incredulity at seeing the airstrip which every six months is flattened for the arrival of the flying doctor; of having been allocated the luxury of my very own theatre mask and hat – disposable in every sense, except that they must last me my two months; of the drug calculations being based on counting the gentamicin vials in Granny's bag; of scouring the hospital to find something with which to rupture membranes; of stoicism observed in too much detail; and of inexplicable hospitality and friendliness in the absence of much of what I had for granted.

As for my purpose: well, it seems that I have to unlearn some things before I can find my true focus. This next week will help.

A Road Ahead Beckons

Whenever I write the word 'mentorship', the spell-check offers me other options – 'mentor's hip'; 'mentor sheep'; etc. The reason is that Mentor was not originally a verb, but a person. (If you have ever been mistaken for a verb, you will know how it feels.) Mentor was, in fact, a wise Greek, who gently looked after the interests of Odysseus's son, Telemachus, while the former was de-Trojaning.

A mentor now is a father figure; a whisperer of wisdom; a nudger of destiny. It was under that guise that I arrived here nearly three weeks ago, and gradually I begin to understand. In one way, my expectations have been realised. One of the Assistant Medical Officers (AMOs) – the delightful Hizza – has recently joined the on-call rota, having only previously performed six solo Caesarean sections. The AMO is the longstop on call – the last player before an unwelcome boundary. My mentorship of his surgical skills has produced a satisfying immediacy of change. He has raw skill, and his self-ratified, sometimes makeshift techniques have not had the chance to become ingrained. He now knows how properly to control a bleeder, how to close a uterus so that it does not look like a Cornish pasty and how to enter the abdomen through the bikini line, a full generation before the arrival of the garment.

As regards the two experienced AMOs, however, I think that I am learning more skills from them than they from me. If that were where it ended, then on return – short of finding myself on hand to wrestle a passing ungulate to the ground – my trip might have been wasted. Mentorship, however, goes beyond the imparting of skill, and steps gingerly on the road to progress. What I am unintentionally bringing, perhaps more than anything else, is an expectation that people might live, and live happily. I am bringing some understanding of how we in the UK expect a maternal death only once in every 10,000 deliveries, where here it is once in every 100 or 50 – or even 30 in the remotest areas.

With regard to baby death, the figures would be even more stark, except that no-one knows them. Most dying babies never arrive at hospital. Some, unsalvageable, tragically do – four this week, for instance. Had I stuck to my idea that mentoring was only boosting the skills of the hospital staff, then how would that have served baby Glory? She was born breech, at night, in the distant fire-lit mud hut of a friendly but foundering traditional birth attendant. A long motorcycle ride later, any

11

hope of saving Glory had been dissipated with each degree of body temperature she lost. No-one cried. No-one does. Perhaps it is the inurement to tragedy that my mentorship might influence most. For the staff, inurement becomes habit, and habit becomes self-fulfilling prophecy:

"This lady needs a Caesarean right away – she has an obstructed labour, and the baby is becoming distressed". (Exit stressed obstetrician stage left, to jostle the theatre team. Thirty minutes pass. Enter same obstetrician looking highly inflammable. Mild groans proceed from a prone figure on a rubber sheet. Muffled chicken noises pass by a rear window.)
"Why is she still here?"
"We are waiting for the laboratory, and the security guard could not find the anaesthetist."
"Please! Come on, let's go!" (Exeunt).

No-one is bad or callous. No-one is meaning to delay. Everyone aspires to an early resolution to the problem. Yet a weary pointlessness sometimes creeps into the bones of the players.

Enter mentorship, stage right. The AMOs have in fact long abhorred the difficulties involved in making things happen quickly when needed. So, prompted by a higher expectation, we talk. We listen. We probe. We explain. We discuss how we might do it differently. The chief AMO calls a meeting of the heads of department, along with me, the AMOs and the hospital superintendent. We explore the options. We resist the temptation to procrastinate. We decide, to my almost worried surprise, that we will set 30 minutes as the maximum time to have elapsed, from making the decision that we have a maternity emergency, to beginning the operation. We adopt a system of monitoring the cause of any lapses. We meet all staff and agree. Three out of the next four Caesareans meet the target.

My unexpected and unenviable job now is to embed and popularise, not just this development, but the whole idea that situations can be improved. Not just that they can be improved, but that a mechanism can be devised for analysing the issues when we don't make it. In the UK, we would call it Significant Event Analysis, and it has been evolving for four or five decades. Here, it has no name and it is as young as that first baby saved.

Forward movement having begun, mentorship is soon going to find itself hard-placed to keep up. Another hospital meeting took place on Friday, again with the overarching hospital boss in attendance, and that was one in which hope for the future took tantalising shape. It began with the excellent Abdallah, the head AMO, presenting his field survey of maternal mortality, and attitudes to hospital birth in the villages we serve. Predictably, most women use the traditional birth attendant (TBA), and 90% of those that arrive at hospital do so with TBA herbs already prodding away at their innards. (Nineteen out of 20 adult hospital admissions have 'peasant' as their recorded occupation.) Abdallah's dream is to reach out to the villages and to build collaboration, mutual understanding and early referral. What makes it more than just hope, however, is the potential contribution of a man whose name is not currently a verb, but should be:

Brad Logan is an American ObGyn who came out just four years ago, to see what he might do to help. Finding the situation that I am now beginning to appreciate, he decided to dedicate his awesome can-do talents to making a difference to rural poverty. The charity Hands4Africa was established and, in the blink of an African eye, one fortunate village has work and money for the first time. Not content with that, he has bradded away, not daunted by circumstance, not accepting impossibility, until his extended goals are beginning to be realised. Water, food, shelter, education, transport – and local health care – have now begun to be tackled in a sustainable way. It is just a beginning for this part of Africa, but an inspiring one. Now he intends to brad five further communities – the very ones whose TBAs we want to reach – and suddenly the prospect of truly working catalytically with traditional communities looks less daunting. Much more of this, I hope, as the story unfolds.

Sion and I even had our gastro-intestinal systems bradded, when the Man of Iron pitched up on our front door step with baskets of actual food. Plus extra-virgin olive oil! Spices! Brown bread! What a hero! Here in Berega, if you know where to look, it is true that you can find food of sorts (unless, it seems, you are either a dog or a female chicken. The former, seemingly immune to the ubiquitous presence of the latter, are mainly dog-bone partly covered in fur. Pets are not a concept which has penetrated very deeply into the Dark Continent. Hens are equally thin, despite the relentless scratching under every bush. Their reluctant ovaries periodically expel what is locally referred to as an 'egg' but is, in fact, one sixteenth of an omelette. Cockerels, on the other hand, seem unreasonably healthy, and shout Gallic jocularities to each other for the couple of hours leading up to the main jamboree at dawn.)

Anyway, food. Yes, you can get it in Berega, but (not counting stuff that comes in sacks), it is all fruit. A bunch of bananas the size of a flock of toucans? 16p. A dozen oranges? 30p. The entire collection of tomatoes displayed on a makeshift counter on a village path? I didn't have a banknote small enough. I had begun to experience the early pangs of ten-a-day poisoning, which presents in the same way as pizza deficiency. My nutrition, now bradded, is fully girded for the challenges ahead.

By the way, I left you with the wrong impression when I said that I was not living with a skillet-wielder. Sion, it turns out, can make an impressive Thai curry out of what I would have regarded as barely compostable materials. It is only fair then, that in return I am passing on to him some surgical skills. On Tuesday, he did his first Caesarean. A large crowd had turned out in the theatre for this planned case, and it was in buoyant mood that we entered the room. Immediately, however, for me alarm bells began to ring: Simon the Zealot was there. Doubting Thomas was there. But where was Peter? Where were the sons of Zebedee? These had become reliable friends in just a short time here, and it was with trepidation that I realised we must undertake the procedure with just two of them.

Just as Jesus only had twelve Apostles, so the hospital has just 12 theatre gowns. They were recruited, one by one, by previous itinerant wise men. They have faithfully served generations of visiting surgeons. Some of them are just rough and rustic, some more sophisticated. All of them you take as you find, but when you need them, they are always there. Except today. It transpired that yesterday's emergencies had used up all, bar Simon and Thomas. (The Iscariot is kept for dirty cases.) At the end of yesterday's procedures, they had all been washed and were now hanging out on the Mount of Olives, behind the theatre block.

Only two gowns left, then, so no scrub nurse – just me and Sion. It went well. Sion has done a couple since, and the current score is Thai curries 3, Caesareans 3. Sion is on call today, so a play-off is imminent.

Let me finish with a theatre gown-related theme. Caesarean section is the beginning of life for as many as a quarter of the population of the planet. When we do one here, we have no clean gowns, no modern sutures, makeshift masks made of bits of muslin, rudimentary

14

anaesthesia, no modern equipment for the resuscitation of the baby, and, well, too many other paucities to count. We even, at the end of each procedure, wash out and recycle the bigger swabs. This parsimony allows us to keep the cost to the woman of a Caesarean at £24 – the monthly salary of a nurse, and an inaccessible fortune to a rural Tanzanian. Thus the need for much bradding. In the new cooperation we hope to foment, we will need to perhaps halve what a woman pays, in order to have fighting chance of encouraging early attendance when problems occur. This needs money. So thanks to those who ventured the sponsored climb of Kilimanjaro. Your death by altitude sickness has not been in vain.

With people like Brad around, maybe this will be the last generation of Tanzanians to endure nature at its harshest.

It remains to be seen, however, whether, by the end of my two months, anyone other than Hizza and Sion will have been Laurenced.

Beginning by being here

I hesitate to tell you my dream for mothers and children in rural Tanzania. Aspiration – yes. Plans – even better. But dream? Dreams are vague. Dreams are frenetic. In dreams, you are at the Old Vic Theatre, supposed to be on stage in two minutes, but you haven't written the play yet, when someone – initially your mum, or possibly your sister, but you gradually realise that it is your biology teacher – comes in to hurry you. You then discover that you have no clothes on, so a friend, who is later a different friend, takes you backstage, which opens onto city rooftops, so that you can fly with him, who is now 'them', pursued by your brother who has got your shoes. When you put them on, you realise they are rugby boots, and your antagonistic nemesis from primary school passes you the ball, and it turns out that you can actually run faster than you can walk, if you didn't need the loo so much, but as you approach the try line, your friendly workmate redirects you onto the stage, where the audience awaits your first words, with increasing disquiet, until you are saved by the fire bell going off so relentlessly that you wake up. (Is it just me that has dreams like this? I've just re-read that paragraph, and even I can see that I need help.)

So a dream is perhaps not the best way ahead when thinking about sustainable development. It is too easy to leap haphazardly hither and thither, prompted by the exigencies and consequences of deep-rooted under-development in this worrying corner of the world. We are beginning, therefore, to collect together our thoughts into an aspiration; and to distil how we might take the first steps in turning that aspiration into reality. Choosing those first steps, however, is not quite as easy as it seems.

When I was in Africa before, I made many mistakes. A characteristic one was to assume that, just because something sounded like a good idea, I was thereby empowered to ram it down the beaks of the chicks in my keeping. A few cuckoos in this way were nourished. A decade and a half later, I was teaching the management of change, on a two-year sabbatical. (On the basis of what qualification, you might reasonably ask? These were the Blair years, I would point out. I looked like I knew. And, more importantly, I knew how to be engaging by not wearing a tie.) So there I was, teaching others what should happen when you unleash a vision statement or Gantt chart or project manager. Dreams would become reality. System development. Admirable and well worked tools.

I had never grasped then, however, and probably still have not now, what actually makes human beings behave in the way that they do. What, for instance, makes you bring a cup of the tea she loves to your darling wife in the morning? Project management? What makes you clear up the Armageddon-like devastation left in the kitchen when you have been cooking, before she sees it? Not Six Sigma. What makes you strongly motivated to ensure that you have completed all the tasks on the list she gave you before she gets home – or at least have a wildly imaginative excuse? Oh, actually that IS project management. Bad example.

The point is this: what really controls behaviour is not so much good ideas, as relationships. It all depends on relationships. I can only sustain positive change in that of which I am a part. So we begin by being here, together, where we are.

But in Africa, where we are is not always a good place.

When I began the maternity ward round on Tuesday morning, I was feeling buoyant. During the night, I had assisted Hizza at two Caesareans, both done with ease and skill using his newly-honed techniques. In each case, the midwife had dealt well with the (anaesthetised) baby, taking account of previous nudgings and admonitions. The second Caesarean, despite being at 5.30am, with an exhausted team, was ready to start within 35 minutes of the call. Very satisfying – and the team were relieved at the lack of time-wasting! Massively satisfying. But when I later arrived on the ward to ask how the first lady was doing, I was told "Fine". She pointed to the woman half way down the ward, un-nursed, lying on her back with an airway in, still deeply unconscious.

"Has she had any observations yet?"
"Yes."
"And…?"
"Blood pressure nil."
"Blood pressure nil?????"
"Yes."
"And she's fine?"
"Yes."

Actually, she was fine. The nurse has just not been able to find the blood pressure because the BP cuff was faulty. Guidelines for post-op care of course exist in Tanzania, but they might as well not, written as they are by someone else, somewhere else. Here, the culture in which we work has been "If you die, you die". That is not neglect; it is the way it is. In the next bed was Joyna. On a previous night, Joyna had made the motorbike journey from Mtumbatu, just 20 bumpy minutes away, in labour in her sixth pregnancy.

Two previous Caesareans had led to two healthy children. We added another to each tally. Three home deliveries, however, had resulted in three stillbirths. Despite this, she had had no antenatal care. A quick survey of the ward showed that more than half of the women with previous pregnancies had had at least one baby die. Indeed, two women on the ward had lost their babies this time round – one to eclampsia and one to congenital abnormalities (her fourth successive child to die at full term). Death is where we are. Whatever the first steps on our journey to a new reality, they will not be the pinning of guidelines on the wall, and the pointing of an angry finger at those who do what they always did.

The first steps then. We have already begun, and my part is tiny, so don't get the impression that I am Gandhi. What I bring is simply knowing that it does not have to be like this, and falteringly imparting this to the staff. The vehicle in which we will be travelling is their belief that it can be different. Slowly, we are gathering an impetus fuelled by getting it right. Emergencies dealt with promptly. Babies well nurtured. Surprising survival, achieved together. Where we hope to be, as soon as we can, is that, in every common mother or baby emergency, we do a good job(mainly), based on the knowledge that we can, and the understanding of how. With that solid beginning, we can think of progress. We plan to engage with the people; with the TBAs; with the 10 births that happen out there for every one that happens in here; with the village health workers and their utter lack of any resources; and with the communities that Hands4Africa will be financially developing, educating, mobilising, and empowering. On Monday, we have a meeting where we will decide the next steps.

By the way, I forgot to mention last week that US President Barack Obama came to visit. Not actually to Berega, and not specifically to see me (as it turned out), but nevertheless he chose Tanzania over his native Kenya to water his flock on his pastoral sojourn across the planet. How strange for me to be just a few hundred kilometres away from the man they call 'the leader of the free world'.

You do get the wonderful feeling of a free world here. As I write, harmony singing is ringing across the valley from the gathering place on the hill. When there is no singing, the chattering of children and the clucking and clicking and cooing fill the spaces with the African sound. The evening fires at the entrances to homes welcome back the workers. Then the stars come out, and the Milky Way is painted in a rough white stripe overhead. It really exists.

For the last five or six nights the moon has simply failed altogether to pitch up but, to be fair to the moon, this has allowed us to see the Milky Way in all its glory. There is even such a thing as starlight. (The other night, I lay in bed in deep darkness. I passed my hand several times right in front of my face, two inches from my nose. I could see absolutely nothing, not even movement. I opened my eyes and it was not much better, but a hint of starlight told me what my hand was up to.)

What else can I tell you of my week? I have lost 6kg already, since landing in Dar es Salaam. If I carry on like this, within a month and a half I shall be back to my birth weight. It may be of course that I have a zoonosis (that is an infestation with a family of nematodes or amoebae) but, if they have a family and I am just an unemployed man of working age, we have to wonder who has more right to be in my body.

I tried to address the weight loss on Wednesday, when the complete lack of any sustenance whatever in our kitchen led me to take the day off and make the two-hour trip to Morogoro. Its market is a wonder. You can get, not just fruit and vegetables, but kettles and cooking pots and string and bags and contraptions and tools for removing leeches from goats' fetlocks and a thousand other things, and then more again.

Innumerable stalls and makeshift displays are rammed into an old colonial shell. Rusty, broken, part-lengths of corrugated iron are woven together into jagged irregular projections of roofing, nailed to crazy wooden frames, to protect the goods from the hot, sweaty sun. (I cannot be sure that the sun sweats, it being a star, but in Morogoro market, it seems to.) There is no fruit you cannot buy – except, bizarrely, apples. Heaps of pawpaw, mango, passionfruit, banana, tangerine, avocado and untold others are laid out in little piles, each pile costing 500 shillings – 20p. (But no Pink Ladies. No Coxes. Nothing makes you want more to be munching on Granny Smith than her total absence.) Then the vegetables, the ginger, the garlic, the tamarind, the cumin, the spices I have never heard of and endless sacks of things to soak for a week before boiling for a couple of hours then throwing away.

In several shiploads, I bought enough for ten-a-day for a decade, and then my reward: protein! At the Morogoro Hotel, I ordered half a chicken, which I reasoned should be enough at least to put weight back on my shoulders, so that I would be able to undo the top button on my shirt without it slipping noiselessly to the ground. Sadly, I had forgotten about East African chickens. When they peck around your door all day, and from time to time perch immediately outside your window to practise crowing for much of the night, they look not-far-off normal-sized. It must be all feather. If you hide a Tanzanian chicken drumstick in a box of matches, you'll never find it again. I duly gnawed the bones, marvelling that these creatures had the strength to walk, far less scrimmage.

And so back to Berega, privileged to be arriving by car, with food. In every direction around, small red mud dwellings, wisps of smoke and noises of evening marked the villages and communities that the hospital serves. Bands of smiling ragamuffins waved us past.

Women with babies on their back and unlikely loads of firewood or well-water on their heads eyed us curiously. The dry river beds and straggling weedy patches of maize in our remoter and higher part of the land contrasted with the rich watered fields around Morogoro.

Might this be the very generation in which we make a different expectation for the people of remote African villages?

We have a dream.

Green Shoots

A newsflash on my nutrition: there has been a touching response to my harrowing, muscle-by-muscle account of the transition from alpha-male silverback into pygmy marmoset, occasioned by eating too healthily. (Perhaps I express it too strongly when I say 'touching'. On reflection, perhaps 'derisive' or 'absent'.) For those who could not have borne the return to Coventry of a withered remnant, mockingly draped in Laurence's skin, I bring good news. Dan.

Dan Towie is Sion's friend – a doctor from England – who has come to stay with us for a couple of weeks to check out Africa, and to be there for Sion. (You would be forgiven for thinking "But Laurence is there for Sion, surely? Is Sion not refreshed to the very marrow by Laurence's admirably detailed and delightfully meandering reminiscences of his (rather more impressive) experience of the same emotional nadir? Does Sion not follow Laurence around, in trembling and breathless anticipation, hoping for yet more of his robustly-delivered snippets of advice and instructions, which so readily fill and soothe the hurting places in the inner soul, displacing all anxiety and uncertainty?" You'd be forgiven, eventually, for thinking that.) Anyway, Dan is here, and completes the spectrum of cooking talent represented in our African home.

At the left-hand end of the spectrum is myself, who is to cooking what Mother Teresa was to basketball.

Considerably to the right of the centre of the spectrum lies Sion, a Tim Henman of the basting pan. Our compost heap is a veritable Henman's Hill.

But, in a spectacular metaphorical leap, the Kaiser of the Kitchen is Dan. Vegetables delight in obeying him, yielding their rough and uncompromising outer antipathy to reveal their inner acquiescence. Spices dance alluringly at his bidding. Even fruits, putting aside ancient enmities, clamour around with legumes and nightshades, waiting to be squeezed, sliced or shredded into masterly culinary victory. The first night – tortilla. Protein! Filling! Delicious! I felt the life creep back into the pecs and six-pack, which so humbly lie a variable distance below the surface. The second night, vegetable curry with spiced soy bean dhal. Soy beans, I would like to remind you, come in sacks, and I had no more considered them part of my nutritional come-back than junk mail. Then on Thursday night, from an unpromising assortment of things-that-used-to-grow, he flourished before us *huevos rancheros*, guacamole and crushed chilli sweet potato! I mean real guacamole! How is this possible!? (Actually, having watched him, I am pleased to be able to report the recipe: take squashy greenish-purple things; flaky white golf-ball things which the previous occupants had left behind; hot crinkly red things which, I discovered, do not work in Nutella sandwiches; squeezes of what I had taken to be last year's quinces; and white salty stuff from a cup labelled 'salt'; do stuff with it; and suddenly, you have guacamole.)

Dan, Sion, Marjan and the remains of me

The nutritional recuperation came as a welcome response to the depressing collection of where-we-are-ness on Tuesday. Before judging too harshly, bear in mind the perspective of a rural African villager. Not much more than 100 years ago in rural Tanzania, there were lions and TB and sleeping sickness and malaria and tetanus and dysentery and hookworm and warring tribes and obstructed labour and colonial oppression and failed crops and droughts and a complete absence of health care; all in the context of scraping around to survive long enough to hope to see the next generation, for the most part. Death was like a weed, finding its way into every corner. This has changed only slowly, and anyone foolish enough to want to tug out every injustice, and take a scythe to all inadequacies, will find him (or her) self tired, and the roots barely harmed. So it is that a rural mission hospital can be overwhelmed if it aspires to perfection – or even, so it can seem, to proactivity. That is a small step from finding itself reacting, slowly, inadequately, only enough to stay where it is. This is not laziness or badness, it is simply a place on the road from the 19th century to the 21st.

And so on Tuesday morning, when Sion had been off for the weekend and the Monday (among a number of other depressing incidents in the day), he experienced:

- a woman admitted to his ward with a late miscarriage four days before, unreviewed since, now becoming very ill with sepsis. (She has now recovered well. This is one of the top five causes of maternal death. On the same day, we dealt with two other conditions from the killer list – obstructed labour and eclampsia. In each case, we did some things well and some things slackly, on this occasion with good outcomes.)
- a baby on its mother's back outside the children's ward, unrecognised as having been ill with meningitis, having seizures.
- the report of a three-year-old child admitted in the night after a fall, very unwell with perhaps a broken leg. Before being seen by the AMO on the morning round, the child died (perhaps from multiple injuries plus preceding chronic illness). This information was given in the hospital's morning report, in the same voice as if the boy had grazed his knee. No-one but us was shocked.

Of course, many other good things had happened. In the historical context, it was just a normal day. Ward staffing is often just one trained nurse, hoping to make some impact where she can, without aspiring to be all-seeing and all-curing.

Sion and I asked for a meeting with the hospital director (Isaac Mgego) and deputy director (Katibu) to explore how we can move more purposefully along the road to progress. We need not – we cannot – solve all the problems at a stroke. We are unable yet, for instance, to influence the advanced state of neglect in which many patients arrive (for instance the child after the fall). We should, however, be able to promise that no-one will die casually in our hospital. We should be able to muster the plentiful but unfocussed good will, and to harness it into targeted activity. We need to recognise the seriously sick and the emergency situations, and deal with them as thoroughly and uniformly as our resources will allow. If we are to engage with communities, and to encourage early referral and attendance with serious problems, then we must be clear that here in the hospital, we deal with those problems assiduously. Many interventions cost prohibitive amounts of money, but carefulness is (almost) free. Can we make this next step?

Of the many determinants of progress in an institution, there is one which matters more than all the others combined: does the boss want it? Isaac and Katibu don't just want it, they are hungry for it – as are many of the staff, so it turns out. They are like seeds in good soil waiting impatiently for the rain, so that they might become green shoots. The rain is just a bit of water. All the goodness is in the seed, and these are good seeds.

Out of our meeting came the idea that we would set out a charter of expectations in dealing with emergencies and the seriously ill; of minimum standards in initial management; promptness; communication; and monitoring and review. Much of this fits neatly with the steps we have already taken to reduce delays in maternity crises. We have slipped a little in this, but not much. Without proactivity we will slip more, but I detect a subtle dissolution of antipathy to this self-imposed harshness. We see (for instance today) a maternity ward where the last dozen emergencies, mostly late referrals who had already been to the TBA, have been dealt with promptly enough to produce 12 thriving babies and 12 healthy mums. Next week, we meet the extended management team to take these ideas further.

That will follow several trips planned for early in the week, where exploration furthers the dream: outreach into five communities; linking to the work being done by Hands4Africa; and, in the fullness of time, having systems for early referral of critical cases. Thereafter, we will need an enhanced front line of Clinical Officers.

The first steps in making that a reality will also be taken next week, when we visit the nearest CO training school, near the capital, Dodoma. I will tell you more of it when I have seen it, but at the moment I continue to be struck by how much the inner areas of the country would still be so recognisable both to Dr Livingstone and to the predators who now limit themselves to the many huge game reserves in the country. This leads me seamlessly to our visit to one of them on Saturday – Mikumi national park.

Of course we were on the look-out for the Big Five: the five most terrifying animals on the planet. Sion saw three of them in the first few hundred yards: mosquitoes, tse-tse flies and me. Everything else would be a bonus. But what a bonus! We stopped at a water-hole (which had a tse-tse fly trap, enabling us to get out of the car. What we had not taken into account was that in getting out, we might let tsetse flies in, fleeing from the trap. One of them showed its gratitude to me later with a kiss, and I anxiously awaited to see if the lip-marks would turn into the characteristic 'eschar', signifying impregnation with sleeping sickness. It didn't, but I've ordered online a new pillow, just in case.)

The water-hole was the size of a football field or so, and, it being the dry season, much of the local fauna was not far away. The most immediately attention-grabbing were the humping hippos, oblivious to the midday heat, taking time out of their busy being-a-hippo schedule to produce some more of the species. Besides ourselves and one other group voyeuring, were a monitor lizard; a variety of crocodiles; a flock of egrets; some Egyptian geese and their impressionable young; a batalla bald eagle (and a juvenile who was just thinning); two fish eagles; six ground hornbills; a herd of buffalo; an extended family of baboons; and five marabou storks.

You cannot begin to imagine marabou storks. They have been recorded as being up to nine feet tall. When they fly, they blot out the sun for a while. It was extraordinary to witness that such birds could heave themselves so effortlessly up into the sky. It reminded me of my rugby career. Today, the reason they did actually heave themselves was, quite unbelievably, that they were mobbed by even taller, but ganglier birds - saddle-billed storks. Presumably their longer reach and defter footwork gave them an advantage, as long as they could avoid a clinch. On the way out, a herd of elephants seemed pretty ordinary in comparison.

As we climbed back along the hot and dusty roads to Berega, it was difficult to tell that we had left the game park, except that the tops of the trees were less nibbled. It struck me that, for a rural Tanzanian grandfather, who was a young man when Mikumi became a National Park, and a little boy when the colonial powers were still the dominant force, the view from his hut would have changed very little. What might be a very welcome sign to him would be some green shoots.

Let's hope that Dan does not make them into *Pousses Vertes Rustiques à la Campagne*.

She ain't heavy

From anywhere to anywhere in Tanzania is a long, long road (if there is one).

The census on everything-you-need-to-know-about-Tanzania has just been published, and please remind me to annexe some of the stats, for any geography students who have strayed onto the wrong book from Ibetyou'reregrettingchoosingthisforAlevel@boringfacts.blogspot.com.

Just to whet your appetite, here are some of the dusty details: the country is humungous. It measures around 900 km by 1,000 km. They haven't yet got around even to begin sorting out great chunks of it. In these areas, hordes of wildebeest trundle and groups of Maasai squat by evening fires, as they have done since wildebeest first said "What are those spiky things squatting by that evening fire, and why are they eating mum?" These areas form the 30-odd national parks and game reserves. The Selous alone – one of the largest game reserves in the world – is about the size of southern England, without the sticky-out bits. In the game reserves, there are no good roads, no service stations and no-one thumbing a lift (for very long).

Perhaps the penning of predators into these vast savannahs is one of the reasons that the population is now expanding at about a million extra people per year. There is still plenty of space, though. Tanzania has lots and lots of wild and wonderful space and surely, one day, a healthy future because of it. Despite the expansion, the current population of the mainland is still only 45 million – less than three-quarters that of the UK. The avoidance of being eaten might be helping the growth, but more importantly, having enough children is a protective response to some grimly depressing factors reflected in the census.

In the rural populations, a household will typically comprise four or five people, and many graves. One in 25 homes has electricity; one in three has safe water nearby; one in 12 has any sort of pit latrine; and more than one in three families subsist below the poverty line. No living children means no living, once past a certain age.

Hamlet on the road from Berega to Tunguli

It is not too surprising then, that the census continues to show that rural Tanzania carries on having one of the worst maternal mortality figures in the world. The best is Estonia, for some reason. (Plenty of fish and an overwhelming desire to produce a Eurovision Song Contest winner?) In Estonia, two women die in every 100,000 live births – an awesome twenty-fold reduction in three decades. In Tanzania, the 2012 figure was 454, making the lifetime chance of dying in childbirth nearly one in 20 women.

It has always been like this here, of course, and people know no different. Indeed, a comparison of the census stats with those from primitive territories with no access to healthcare, reveals that it would not be much worse if no hospitals existed in much of the isolated areas. The reason is simple: no hospitals exist in much of the isolated areas.

On Monday, we went to visit one that actually is there – Mvumi. It was our first trip further inland, and we had to pass through the capital of Tanzania, Dodoma. From our hospital, it is about 20 minutes to the main road, and then a bit more than a two-hour drive to Dodoma. (More still if you get stuck behind a convoy of trucks headed for the deep interior – even more if you get squashed by one. In Tanzania, a dual carriageway is where a bike with innumerable 25-litre water containers tied into a Santa's sackload can overtake another bike with a small copse of charcoal-grilled saplings balanced across the back wheel, without having a head-on collision with a motorbike taking an extended family to market with their spare goat.)

On the way, we pass through Gairo, the only town other than our own, in the 263 km between Morogoro and Dodoma, to have a hospital. They bid to become the District Hospital, for which they will had to fix the fact that they had no doctors, no AMOs, no transport and no Caesarean facility. Gairo looks just like a town from the Wild West – ox carts, a single wide main dirt road with a single turning and frontages of entrepreneurial shops – hardware stores, barber shops, iron- mongers, mop-and-bucket outlets and makeshift eateries. It just needed tumbleweed and Gary Cooper. We stopped at the Rusty Axle Corral to get our tyres checked, and I kept look-out for Lee van Cleef.

From Gairo on to Dodoma, the thing that struck me most was the lack of turnings. I don't just mean motorway junctions, I mean turnings – any turnings. Every 20 kilometres or so, a grubby finger would point down a packed-earth track and say something like 'Chagongwe 71km'. You get the feeling that they would be 71 challenging kilometres, and you hope that Chagongwe would be worth it. If you were to look back at your various map and GPS sources, you would find that there is actually just one road: east to west, Morogoro to Dodoma, and then on to Rwanda. For a county or two north and south, there is nothing except barely recognisable dry-mud tracks. Just one tar road – point the car towards it, and you will end up in Dodoma. (A lack of navigational complexity which is my wife's driving dream. Or at least would be, once the car is facing in the right direction:

"Darling, I really don't think this is Barcelona – the road signs are in Swedish. Are you sure we turned right at France?")

Dodoma will one day be a much sought after place to live. At 3,700 feet, it has the perfect climate. It is the seat of parliament, has two major universities, is at the centre of the country, is throbbing with life, has an enormous central fruit and spice market and has places to sit and drink tea in the gentle, dry warmth of the morning sun.

But Dodoma is still very young, and is about as cosmopolitan as the Outer Hebrides in winter. In an hour of taking it in, we saw one Arab, one Asian, and two people in the distance who, by their shorts, sunglasses, safari hats and glistening factor-50-besmeared skin, might have been European. We stopped for a bite to eat, and were given a menu … but were told that nothing on it was available, so we wandered around until we found another café. There, we made our own coffee from flasks of hot water, then tucked into chapati and banana, not risking the chicken soup. I had been lulled into thinking that the gas cooker was the source of the chapati, but as you picked your way through the back yard to the loo, there was an open fire on the ground, and something was baking in an ancient pan. Hopefully not a previous customer.

Mvumi hospital is about an hour's drive from Dodoma. Even though I am more used to Tanzania now, I could not readily assimilate the idea that the main road out of the capital city to the nearest main hospital, is only surfaced for the first mile.

Thereafter, yellow clay became red packed-dirt. You could sense that a hot sun beats down on this high plateau for much of the year. Mountains formed a distant surround, and the countryside featured scattered cacti, scrubby bush, brave but stunted acacia and bizarrely-shaped humps of rock, presumably flung out during a primeval subterranean altercation. Mvumi hospital itself was the size of a large village, or even a small town. We were met by some of the happy and inspiring team that lead, not just the hospital, but the training of Clinical Officers. COs are the level below AMO (themselves the level below medical doctor). COs are the medical front-line in Tanzania. A three-year course, and a school-leaver is ready to triage the sick and dictate the initial management of everything from aardvark bite to zoonosis. Quite incredibly, this unassuming institution, seeing the vast need in this vast terrain, in a few years has gone from self-funding mission hospital to (mission-led) government-funded District Hospital, where no fewer than 150 Clinical Officers are in training. They helped us hugely in our quest to plan the future training of COs at Berega, and we left with half a terabyte of curricula and protocols, as well as much inspiration and plentiful tea.

On the way back, the full moon rose at sunset, and tried to pretend that it hadn't been shirking for much of the previous month. Driving the long road back by the light of the moon (and the headlights, thankfully) was an almost eerie experience. Out there was Africa in the raw. From time to time, Maasai on the side of the road would whip in their cattle, still uncomfortable with the intrusion of the last century or two.

On Friday night, I treated my first Maasai. Few come to hospital for childbirth, but this young girl was brought by her mother because of headache and profound swelling of the face and legs. Of course, she had severe pre-eclampsia. She had no idea how far pregnant she was, but I guessed around 28 weeks. She seemed adolescent, but Maasai do not seem to count age in years. We initiated therapy, but the only way to stop the process before it kills the mother is to deliver, and our neonatal unit consists of a slightly warmer room with no cots, and four mums' beds packed rather too close to each other.

The girl's mother was striking: tall, lean and deep black in colour, but with almost European features. Smooth, unwrinkled skin, despite a few grey hairs. Thick-soled bare feet with toes splayed like fingers, as they are in humans who don't wear shoes. A thin layer of dirt on much of the strong but feminine arms, but no unwashed odour, except perhaps one of good earth. Her ears were pierced to receive ornaments the size of cotton-reels, and round her neck were layers of white-toothed strings. Protecting the wrists and ankles were many-ringed spirals of gold-coloured bracelet. Three lengths of characteristic Maasai coloured cloth were knotted in various ways around her body to form her garment.

There followed the uncanny experience of four languages. I tried to explain in English to the nurse, that we needed to transfer the girl to where the baby might survive. The nurse was Kaguru-speaking but, reverting to the common parlance of Swahili, was able to get the message across to the mother, who transmitted snippets to her daughter in the Maasai tongue. The message I got back was that the father had gone to sell a cow to pay for treatment, and would not be here until the morning, so transfer was out of the question. We repeated the magnesium and blood pressure treatment, and did not need to tell the girl's mother to sleep under the bed and watch her overnight, as that is where all the women's mothers sleep in our ward. Of course, the girl did later have a fit, which was almost a relief as I dreaded the idea of sending such a time-bomb so far, for potentially so unlikely a benefit. We did the Caesarean this morning. The girl's mother sat on the grass outside the theatre block, waiting to receive the child, who we knew was not for this world. In traditional Maasai culture, a birth is not even recognised for the first three months of life, because death is so common.

This Caesarean experience was in stark contrast to the rest of the week – and indeed the month. Although sometimes slipping in the aim to get things moving promptly in obstetric emergencies, we have generally got it right. Last night, I did my second successful Kiwi for malposition, delightfully easy, and saved a weepingly grateful mother of three the expense and morbidity of a Caesarean. Until yesterday, we had not had a single death all month from obstructed labour. (Our normal tally of baby deaths at birth has been about one in every 11 births, amounting to sometimes more than a dozen deaths a month.) But yesterday we did slip. In the busy, yet casual, ill-structured day of the maternity block, somehow a mother managed to be in labour for ten hours before anyone noticed. We have yet to find out whether it was because the staff do not have the routines to ensure that such events do not occur, or whether the mother was coaxed to the hospital perimeter, as happens, to be given illicit doses of labour-enhancing tea. Between dawn and 3pm, the baby died of obstructed labour.

By a strange irony, it was yesterday morning that the hospital director had called the follow-up meeting to last week's exploration of how we might, systematically, do better. In attendance were the next layer down of three bosses of staff, plus myself, Sion, Dan and the director and deputy. I need not have worried about how I was going to gently tease the idea of standards into the conclusions. The excellent Mr Mrase, head nursing tutor, pointed out early in the meeting that the only way we could hope that staff would uniformly live up to expectations was to make those expectations explicit in the standards to which we should be working. Hooray.

Perhaps I should feel a little more guilty than I do about being an (admittedly charming and likeable) European swanning in and telling everyone what to do. I excuse it partly because I try to disguise it, with a subtlety akin to Mike Tyson asking you if you might want to let him go ahead of you in the queue, or would you prefer never to walk again. But also, I am pushing at an open door. Many people are ready for making Berega as good as it can be, and are relieved that an outsider can come and take the blame for letting in the wind of change.

There is much that will not change quickly, and perhaps does not need to. The Mount of Olives behind the theatre block will still flap with the recently-washed 'apostles' hanging on the line. The chickens will peck at the bits of food left by the relatives who have make-shift camps in the hospital quadrangle. A waiting mother will still cook *ugali* porridge in an old iron pot on an open fire outside the waiting mothers' hut.

But at least she is waiting here, not somewhere out there in that huge country. At last, she might reasonably expect that we are working towards making her childbirth journey safer than it has ever been.

But as I look out from my house on the hill to the distant cars on their way to Dodoma, it strikes me that it is a long, long road.

Yellow chuck-chucks

Yesterday, Mama Liz told me off for throwing a few old bottles and empty tin cans into the rubbish pit. Of course, rural Africa has no mechanisms for dealing with waste so, until now, in a system akin to A&E triage, we have had a three-way disposal plan for garbage:

- combustible materials that don't produce a pall of rancid smoke choking the life out of Mother Earth, we burn mercilessly.

- plant waste – the 2 kg of tomatoes you never got round to using; peelings of wizened sweet potato (peeled with a knife, to leave behind Lowry-sized remnants for cooking); the inedible parts of the bruised papaya you bought cheaply last week; the edible parts of the bruised papaya you bought cheaply last week; mango stones and peel, plus all the bits of flesh that aren't inextricably woven into your incisors; the outsides of guacamole; yellow things that you never knew what they were and didn't dare eat – these, and the like, we put on the compost heap, in the ridiculously optimistic expectation that, in two years, compost will magically appear from what was not eaten by the monkeys, ants, termites, chickens, rodents, fruit flies and what I take to be anti-compost beetles. (Indeed, an enterprising bush baby has actually set up a small market stall next to the pathetically penetrable walls of the would-be compost mountain.)

- non-degradable waste – old washing-up liquid bottles (the contents of which, in this country by the way, only leave your hands as soft as your face if you have previously dipped your face in bitumen then dried it with a blow-torch); glass; tin cans etc – we have been in the habit of throwing into the pit, where they await the inevitable.

Not so inevitable, Mama Liz says. In Africa, things have many uses and (if not living) many lives. In the UK, everyone's cupboard-under-the-sink is full of the bottoms of Tupperware containers and the tops of different-sized ones. In rural Tanzania, however, there are no Pound Shops and no plethora of containers. If you want somewhere to store your old bits of soap, what better than a recycled tin can? A glass peanut-butter jar is a candle stand. Beer-bottle tops become an abacus. If you make sunflower seed oil (out of sunflowers, as it turns out), then old water bottles are perfect for storage. Even the washing-up liquid bottle has an unlikely future, as a squeezy container for zapping termites as they try to gnaw into the tired door frame of the family home. Waste not, want not. OK then, this is Tanzania – perhaps just waste not. Africa re-sets your thermostat.

It is not only detritus which has multiple potential uses, but also everyday possessions. Chickens, for instance. They can turn pecked-at used-corncob into egg; they can warn you of danger; they can remind you that it is dawn; they can remind you that it is only one hour until dawn; they can remind you it is only two hours until dawn; they can turn floating carrots into chicken soup; they can add a clucking, chooking, scratching back-beat to the rhythm of rustic African life; and they can be used as currency by the poor to pay, for instance, for a traditional birth attendant. Today's chicks are tomorrow's birth-price.

This came home to me powerfully on Tuesday's visit to Nhembo (pronounced 'Nhembo'). The previous night we had had a rainstorm of sorts, and so the road was damp and slippy. (Old folks here say that, in the days when all between these mountains was low forest, we would often have rain in winter. As the trees left, so did the rain.) We took the back road out of Berega, into the big beyond. Small mud villages slipped by, with antiquity only momentarily challenged by our passing. After five or six kilometres, we found a side-turning and we tossed and tumbled down the slope to a river crossing. Women were washing clothes, somehow not swapping new dirt for old. The dry-season rain had left just six inches of water, but the semi-vertical banks challenged even our trusty ancient Land Rover. Abdallah, driving, told me that recently he had got stuck in this river, and the nurses had got out and pushed. They had thereafter conducted the clinic with one eye on the sky, but eventually arrived home safely.

Arriving home safely, however, is surely not a reliable turn of events on the other side of this river. We drove for an hour altogether, and eventually pulled in by a dilapidated bare building, which turned out to be the local church for half a dozen hamlets around. The tin roof rattled gently on the red clay-brick walls. Inside, a couple of dozen home-made benches were not much more than rough planks on stubby legs. The only other furniture, a rickety kitchen-table altar, had been commandeered as the nurses' station. The glass-free windows, all of different shapes and heights, looked out on straggly patches of crops assailed by the inevitable bush, with the mountains distant yet impressive. A tiny shed stood off at a respectful distance in a field, ready to be of service in longer sermons.

Outside, I had expected a trickle of women and children to arrive for their antenatal checks, immunisations and growth-charting. In fact, more than 100 women, plus their (mainly thriving) offspring stood around chatting, laughing, milling. A few women sat under the acacia tree selling bananas and *mandazi* dough balls. I bought a bunch of small bananas with a 20p (500-shilling) note, and the woman later dashed after me with the 16p change.

It was an awesome tribute to some unknown community health warrior that immunisation and growth-charting was clearly so deep-rooted. But what of childbirth? Where did they deliver? Who did the deliveries? How did they get to hospital if it rained? Abdallah began talking to one of the mums: six children. All delivered here by the TBA. And you mama? Four children. Delivered in that small village over there. And you mama? Three children, all quick deliveries. The traditional birth attendant barely had time to arrive and claim her chickens.

But what if there are problems? Then they come to Berega. How much does it cost? TSH 5,000-shillings on a *piki piki* (motorbike) is the normal price but, when you are in trouble in labour and need to go with your sister mounted behind you, the price is TSH 20,000. What if it rains? You come back. What if you don't have TSH 20,000? You don't go. We didn't have the heart to ask the other questions.

Nhembo is only half-way to the edge of our territory. Chagongwe is the furthest point, another 20 km on a worsening road, and then up the mountain. Our ambition is to reach out to villages like Chagongwe and begin the conversations that might eventually lead to maternity care at last being available. Initially a (maternal-child health) community health worker will be sent out for talking and listening. What happens at the moment? What do they feel that they need? Who are the leaders? Who the potential health workers? We need to meet the TBAs and get their view on the past, the present and the future. There will be no blueprint that tells us how to engage, how even to begin, except simply to start the conversations.

We can promise nothing as yet, but we have hope. Chagongwe, for instance, is one of the communities that Hands4Africa is intending to reach, ultimately with economic opportunity, transport and education. If we can gradually blend health into the mix, then perseverance might lead us to local solutions. If, at the same time, we begin a Clinical Officer training programme at Berega, then we stand a chance of being able to deal with the wave of work we unleash.

The Clinical Officer training programme raises for me an important philosophical question. How many *wazungu* do we bring in? (Europeans are called '*wazungu*'. Originally a term of mixed respect and awe, it now means something between 'people in shorts who forget to greet you, and then ask to take a photo' and 'people who turn up to meetings on time in a bad mood'.) Post-colonial Africa gradually realised that the popping in and out of *wazungu* could do more harm than good. Deeply-caring figures of authority dictating the right way; intolerant tolerance; creation of dependence; blurring of identity; cajoling by the culturally-insensitive yet well-intentioned; then suddenly an exasperated absence, and a regression to the mediocre. The culture clash has not been all one-sided, and of course those oppressed in the past by colonialism have sometimes exaggeratedly resented the intrusion of the erstwhile oppressor.

But are we emerging into a new day? Post-post-colonialism? A generation has passed, and it seems to me now that we both know who we are. I look at the wealth of talented, healthy baby boomers in England, the very ones who marched the streets in their youth to protest at the colonialism of their fathers – or at the very least listened to music that their parents disapproved of, while under the influence of things their parents disapproved of. Are we not now all on the same side? Well, that may be a little naïve, but I'm OK with naivety. When we have the Clinical Officer training, then, can *wazungu* of various disciplines take it in turns to come over and enhance the training, as long as the base is solidly Tanzanian? Here they really want it. Can English-speaking primary teachers not come and help in Mama Liz's school for a month or two? She really wants it. I think we might be ready for a spot of post-postcolonial-*wazungu*-ism.

With regard to this particular *mzungu*, however, my impact, as measured by body weight, is now once more on the decline. Having been boosted by the culinary dexterity of Dan the Mighty, I am now thrown on scarcer resources. Thankfully, Sion is still there, and last night conjured an impressive lentil stew from the unlikely ingredients of lentil and stew. But he works very hard and cannot always be looking out for me. As I sit at the desk all day writing this, I am painfully aware that my ischial tuberosities are protruding through my flesh and impaling themselves on the chair. Let me have bums around me that are fat. Sleek-bottomed bums and such as pad the seat. My buttocks have a lean and hungry look. They ache too much. Such bums are dangerous. (If you don't understand that last bit, ask someone who went to school when they still had inkwells.)

On Wednesday then, having missed early breakfast, I came back late morning and decided to whip up a Spanish omelette. Well, let's say something in between English and Spanish. A Santander ferry omelette, maybe. Anyway, it had some onion in it, as well as other traditional ingredients such as egg. I was proud of myself, and served it up on our last piece of brown bread.

I particularly needed the nutrition on Wednesday, because we had the follow-up meeting to last week's, on making a charter of expectations, to set standards for working in the hospital. I have said that I am naïve, but even I do not believe that a magic new day will dawn tomorrow and dissolve the problems of the past like morning mist. A charter of standards will not create excellence overnight. But what is surely true is that, without it, we will remain in the dark. There were too many examples this week of the nocturnal insufficiency of current practice: delays; casualness; tolerance of the unacceptable; death as a travelling companion. On the other hand, there were many other examples of diligence, caring and dedication in sometimes the most depressingly desperate of circumstances. As I write this on Saturday night at 8 o'clock, more of the senior staff are in the hospital than are at home.

The excellent news is that, on Wednesday, we agreed, including all of the management, that we would take a charter of standards to the staff. We would indeed sign up to a charter, however battered and tattered, of minimum standards. The amazing Sion, I hope, will gently, warmly and persistently be trying to make the children's ward a showcase. I cannot imagine anyone more suited for the job (aided by another worthy *mzungu* – David Curnock – who came the following month). We need plenty of others, as naïve as we are, to see it through.

The final *mzungu* to mention is Marjan, who arrived on the scene from Belgium, via four months in Ethiopia. Marjan is a lab person and, in just a few days, has opened up for me a whole new vista: lab staff on ward rounds who help, advise and then quickly give you answers to the questions you might have had. What a resource. Like Dan, she is just here for three weeks, but is like a shining light.

The future, then, is beginning to take more shape. A hospital where death is unwelcome. Caring wards where good work leads to fewer problems. All joining together, including *wazungu*, in the shaping of this and in the development of Clinical Officer training, to root deeply a culture of learning and striving.

Then, for mothers and their babies, we will begin outreach to the unreached villages and invite cooperation. We will invite them to deliver more safely in our safer hospital. We will go back with them into the community and help ensure that their babies grow into healthy children. Within five years, we hope that the mothers of those villages will have other uses for their chickens.

Imperfect Instruments

In the small hours of the morning of Thursday 8 August 2013, I saw what I expect will be my last womb (barring, perhaps, when I am finally put into Fort Semolina retirement home, getting allocated the bathchair opposite a naturalist with prolapse).

It was a blessing that my last-ever action as a doctor was an operation – and that my last-ever operation was assisting in a Caesarean. Like the seasoned night-club bouncer on the door of the Wonky Innards, I have grappled far too often with unwelcome visitors, bustling them to the abdominal door and thence into the hands of the waiting pathologist. How much nicer to find that the ruckus was due to a little baby crying with joy at the prospect, finally, of meeting the outside of his mum.

A wriggly boy, who had struggled to be born in a long labour, responded heart-warmingly to being vigorously dried and wrapped, and thereafter greeted his weary mother with one of life's most beautiful sounds. Welcome to the world, little baby.

Hizza was the surgeon, and it was to be our last operation together. The operation was performed, as always in Berega, with imperfect instruments – needle-holders that, in an irony lost on them, no longer hold needles; old-fashioned sutures; torn drapes; gowns with one cuff missing; over-tolerant scissors that only cut after three final warnings; a catheter the size of a hose. The surface on which the game was played, instead of being softly-surfaced memory-foam, was an ancient, hard table, rudely covered with an even more ancient rubber sheet. Nevertheless, Hizza made a good fist of it. He did a horizontal incision instead of his previous vertical; he remembered to make a double-bite stay on each angle; to leave these knot-ends on a clip; and all traces of Cornish-pastyness had been eliminated from a precisely-executed double-layer closure of the uterus. Nice job.

I am sure that he will not mind if I say that, not long ago, he also was an imperfect instrument, the product of his circumstances. He had had sparse, if any, one-to-one supervision in his surgical training, and what he knew was what he had gleaned and inferred. His eagerness to entice every last tip and nuance of surgery out of me before my final day was touching and humbling. I felt that if he now performs as many thousand Caesareans as I have, then it will truly have been my privilege to have been there for him in his early days. This alone was worth crossing a few continents for.

Of course, he is not yet perfect. The fact that perfection is an unattainable goal means that both he and I will always be imperfect instruments (although I am surgically less imperfect now than at my first abdominal operation in 1976. It was an appendicectomy. I remember it vividly, not just because it was my first, nor because it took so long that I could barely remember life before it began; nor due to the resultant stress perhaps being the origin of the challenge to my scalp which has blighted my barber's life ever since, and is perhaps the reason why surgeons wear hats. But principally because, in those days, you learned by watching, rather than by being taught. And so, when I asked if I could do this appendix, the senior registrar said "Have you done one before?" "No." "OK. Well you can do this one, but I'll wait in the coffee room so that I don't put you off".)

Since then, I have got better, but never perfect. There must be a book or two in there (or more probably already out there, as are most of the stories that I otherwise would have written), on the paradox that purposefulness is the pursuit of the unattainable, and futility is the pursuit of anything else.

It is for the purpose of making doctors less imperfect that the new regulations of appraisal and revalidation are currently being implemented. I fully concur. When my revalidation date comes up soon, I will not have the evidence of 250 hours of ongoing education in the last five years; nor the organised reflections of patients and colleagues on my work; nor the five annual appraisals of my strengths, weaknesses, needs and plans; nor the plethora of filled-in forms. Apart from the last of these, the other elements are truly are good, and the day that I start to believe that my experience makes me exempt, is (was) the day that I should retire. (The world is a better place because of Lord Lister, without whom many millions would have died of peri-operative sepsis. But if he were alive today, aged 186, I wouldn't let him within 20 stretcher-poles of me if I were to need an op.)

And so, 41 years 10 months and a few days after stepping up to Liverpool Medical School, eager and young, bursting with possibility, and blessed with a strong liver, I lay down my stethoscope. Ana after tens of thousands of operations, and tens of thousands of childbirths, I now also hand in my scalpel and exchange it for a pen – which, to be honest, is less likely to cut my hand.

The week that ended with a life-saving operation had begun with the tragic absence of one. Sion and I were on-call last weekend and a 23-year-old woman was brought in from afar with abdominal pain and collapse. White as death, she died in front of us before we had a chance even to begin the search for a donor of blood. She might have had a ruptured spleen secondary to malaria, in which case she would have been difficult to save. But it was harrowing to think that it might have been as simple as a ruptured ectopic pregnancy, instantly curable by a simple operation, if we had seen her half an hour earlier.

The rest of the weekend brought many other challenges. Perhaps the most spectacular success was Sion's clinical diagnosis of massive lung pathology in a child of 11. X-rays showed a complete white-out of the right side. Subsequent repeat pleural aspirations over the next few days (tolerated with impressive and characteristic courage) eventually eliminated 1.3 litres of pus from the grateful boy's pleural cavity. He is doing very well, but hides when Sion approaches.

During the weekend, there were other deaths as well – one from cancer at one end of life, and one from meningitis at the other. But yet others were rescued by Sion, sometimes impossibly so – a baby with pneumonia whose oxygen levels were under 60% is now recovering well. (The mum's comments will be one for the appraisal folder.) Anyway, Sion – you made a difference. The totality of suffering in the world is just a bit less.

As you will have doubtless inferred from reading thus far, when writing these reminiscences, I like to ooze effortlessly from paragraph to paragraph, forging unlikely links with literary dexterity. And so it is with suction cup extraction.

I brought Kiwi suction cups to Africa, wondering whether the 20 that Nicholas nobly fast-ferried from Cardiff would be enough. As it was, I only used four in two months, during which time I performed or assisted at 70 Caesareans for obstructed labour. Their use in these cases still emphasised their irreplaceable importance in Berega-like settings, but I am perplexed by the rarity of need there. I brought forceps, but did not use them once. Furthermore, I did not see a single case of PPH (post-partum haemorrhage), the world's number-one killer of mothers. By contrast, first-stage obstructed labour was a daily occurrence. I could annexe a page of musings on this for the childbirth professionals and the curious.

I can talk with despot-like confidence of annexing, because I am writing this from Dar es Salaam. Not only does my computer now say that I have internet but, much more importantly, it also behaves as if I do. Soon you will be able to see the hospital and the environs through the inestimable wonders of YouTube and the WorldWideWeb.

One of the joys of the net, besides being able to read my emails more than one word at a time, is that I have finally been able to check out the workings of the knitted-baby-hat charity Kofia. Blanché, Debbie and the worthies of Guildford, I salute you! Starting with just goodwill, knitting needles and a wireless router, you have begun a process which has the potential to enhance the outcomes of childbirth for people who have never known anything other than fate. The babies' hats are truly a wonderful and welcome intervention. Getting cold is the biggest threat to a baby struggling to adapt to its first few minutes outside the womb. Berega cannot afford proper baby towels, and the knitted hats will send a message of loving warmth from one world to another.

More importantly still, I am hoping that when these baby hats go home to the hamlets, they can be a powerful sign of how much we would like to reach out to those current beyond access. On my last day at the hospital, the key players met, and we have a plan for the first year of outreach to the community. Working alongside Hands4Africa and their plans for community development and transport, I believe that we have a real chance of starting something really important. We will begin cautiously and take each step gingerly. We will seek first to understand. We will try to measure. The purpose is not to do things to people, but to create harmony of purpose. Synergising the efforts will be slow. Traditional birth attendants, making a hard-won and inadequate living from bringing the next generation into the world, need to be our local partners, and that will be a long journey. A journey, once begun, however, will always lead to somewhere more interesting than your front room.

Nowhere was this more true than my last journey from Berega. (A better link this time?) Leaving the hospital after two months was strange. We set off at 6.30am, just in time to see the new moon rise for Eid. (I can only hope that the joy with which it was greeted will encourage a more regular attendance by this recalcitrant lump of rock in future.) For a while at least, I had my last powdered milk cup of tea. Our last banana breakfast. The last "News of the morning?" greeting to the gateman (the answer to which is always "Good!", even if one of the four horsemen of the Apocalypse had stabled at your home the night before. No more Caesareans at which the mother calls her child after me (even if she spells it 'Rollent'). My last time to hear "*Shikamoo!*" (a greeting of respect to elders) from children on the long walk to school.

I have four more days in Dar to finish putting things on the 'web, and to put on some of the lost two stone (assuming that the current population of protozoa in my intestines can be eliminated when the pharmacies open tomorrow). It feels unsettling to be unleashed back into the other world, but it is a very welcome unsettlement.

When I look back at these two months, we have made a good start. The meeting of senior staff and management with the leads of the clinical areas introduced to them the idea of agreed minimum standards of the hospital. I had anticipated a bloody battle, and a long, hard meeting. Well, the meeting was certainly long (and all in Swahili), but that was because the staff themselves punctuated every point with their own tales of how vital it was to build that standard into established practice. Rules are important in Tanzania, and lack of their being explicit has, it transpires, been unwelcome to many. The entire document got through with just a few additions, and no deletions. Berega has a charter.

A final reflection: you may have been surprised the first time that I discussed Berega hospital's flaws, as well as its challenges. There is so much good in the hospital: sound lead clinicians, many dedicated and talented staff and excellent managerial leadership. I wondered if it was acceptable to reflect on inadequate responses, and even to hint at what sometimes seemed too much like neglect. However, I decided that I needed to give you the story as it really is. However much better Berega is than it has been in the past, however much it is head-and-shoulders above many of the District Hospitals in the rural areas, nevertheless it is true that bad outcomes in the hospital sometimes owed as much to its inadequacy as to its inaccessibility to those in distant communities.

Berega has been, like me, an imperfect instrument.

The tragedy of the hedgehogs

Just over a week ago, still full of Africa, I landed on an unaccustomed green island, a bit befuddled and bemused. In the airport, hordes of my tribe jostled and jabbered. Then, like ducklings crossing a road, they self-organised into a wavy line to negotiate passport control. The English seemed instinctively to know who had arrived first, and this unwritten law wielded an awesome power, woe-betiding any would-be self-advancement. It felt strangely foreign. At the baggage carousels, I tried to find my previous impatience, but it never appeared, presumably lost in transit. I grappled my 40 kg of luggage from the belts, trying to remember why I had brought so many pairs of trousers and yet only two legs.

Then, as is customary for the English, nothing to declare, and so through to England. Aaaaaaaah, England! Thanks for waiting for me. A fresh breeze. Damp, leaf-green trees and vivid, bright green grass. Why would I have missed grass? It hadn't missed me. I am struck first with gratitude to be back, and then with curiosity as to why it should matter so. Wasn't the weather better in Tanzania? Wasn't the pace of life less frantic? Weren't even strangers there kind and welcoming, with a shared chuckle at my mangled Swahili? Why would I prefer a cloudy sky with a hint of rain? Do Tanzanians arriving home have the same sense of grateful relief at the first hot whiff of Dar es Salaam dust, or the first iron taste of cauldron-cooked *ugali*? What is home, that it beckons so powerfully? I had only been away two months, and you could get more than that (if the magistrate were in a bad mood) for vexatious tort in fief. I am part of the first generation of a tiny proportion of humanity never to have suffered enforced and prolonged absence from home, and I don't think that I quite appreciate my good fortune.

I climbed into the back of the car, revelling in the tarmac surface, the lack of roll-bars and the absence of dog, cow, chicken and impala dents on the bodywork. From the radio, I caught the end of a programme: "… sadly, that's the tragedy of the hedgehogs". Apparently our spiny chums, seemingly incapable of internalising the essentials of road safety, are dwindling in numbers. This, it transpires (unless you are an ant or part of the pro-grub lobby) is bad news. I could not help dwelling on our separate understanding of the idea of tragedy.

As we cruised along the familiar A45, (Oh the wonderful A45!), I could not extinguish my relief to be home, even with thoughts of the tragedies I had seen. It needed a prickly comparison to bring home to me the privilege of my circumstances. Soon I would be eating a Taylor's Welsh Dragon sausage. I would be drinking a glass of Malbec in our comfortable home, in our comfortable neighbourhood, surrounded by my healthy family and friends, in our peaceful countryside (albeit made more peaceful by lack of hedgehog revelry). What a blessing!

I arrived home, the door was flung open and I was hugged into the house. Five minutes later, I was pouring real, liquid milk into a cup of tea. (I knew it hadn't just been an imagined memory.) Then, joy! Freddie, my one-year old grandson, toddled in and eyed me intently, brow deeply furrowed, for a full few minutes. This was a moment I had feared: would he remember me? We had been so close before. Now, however, not only had I lost a lot of weight, but also I had adorned the physiognomy with a smart, closely-trimmed, attractive, designer beard. ("You haven't bothered to shave" seems to me a much harsher way of expressing it, especially when shaving in Africa was a waste of two precious minutes of sleep before the 7.30am start.) When looked at from the right angle, my resemblance to George Clooney or Sean Connery's much younger brother was now uncanny. After several soul-searching minutes, Freddie's brow unfurled, a big smile unfolded, and the arms lifted towards me for a long, long where-have-you-been cuddle. Home!

My wife Mis came back from work that evening and we met outside on the path. This year, we have been together for 40 years and, in all that time, this was the longest we had been apart. Our eyes met and – maybe I'm reading too much into that deep and unspoken gaze, but – it seemed to say, "At last! Someone to mend the bathroom tiles!" I jest, of course and, for the soppier readers of this book, I have to admit to a slight moisture in the eyeballs, at seeing my lovely wife again. After just two months! How mad is that?

"So what was it like?" someone asked. How could I sum it up in a word? I decided on "Big." That seemed to do the trick and, as no-one asked for further amplification, willing messengers were then despatched, one to the frying pan and another to the wine rack.

The next morning, sausaged and Malbec-ed to the gunwhales, I had time to reflect on what next. There is a long road ahead, but staying where we are is just not an option, even if it were wanted. The world is striding ahead apace. While I was in Berega, electricity arrived. I was there for the first Caesareans done without the background hum of the generator. Roads were being built. Concordats were being signed. There were even plans for water to be piped from the lakes to the dry, high centre. One of the most bizarre developments was even ahead of systems in England: last month Berega began to pay salaries using mobile-phone money: credit that you can then text to any other mobile phone. In June, staff used to take the three-hour bus ride each way and the two-hour bank queue, to pick up their monthly salary in hard cash. In July, they could buy a kilogram of rice in the mud-hut village store by mobile phone credit transfer.

Progress is happening. Change is coming, and we have to be moving. Once the anchor is up and the sail is set, the wind might blow us where we need to be. Mothers and their babies must not be left behind.

We have a plan, so let's just begin and see where that leads. At the Tanzanian end, we have the utmost commitment from the hospital bosses, and determination in the direction of travel – as evidenced by the new charter of standards in the hospital. We have a number of volunteers lining up for future medical involvement with the hospital. Most of all, however, we have a daily tragedy unfolding which, with a little effort and some limited resources, we can begin to tackle.

If we can find the support, we can transform our chosen isolated village of Mnafu from being a distant and inaccessible place where women and children needlessly die, to one where they have a realistic chance of a healthy future.

Progress might be as simple as engagement with the community, and a gentle introduction for them to the 21st century. The worst that can happen is that we fail.

Beautiful, distant and inaccessible

Post Script

Ah the joy of fast internet! Herewith some now downloaded links:

Road to Mnafu: http://youtu.be/cDGP2GJRWuA
http://www.youtube.com/watch?v=cDGP2GJRWuAfeature=youtu.be

Hospital House: http://youtu.be/n84o3Mztf9o
http://www.youtube.com/watch?v=n84o3Mztf9ofeature=youtu.be

Berega Hospital: http://youtu.be/D9YBOYn10FA
http://www.youtube.com/watch?v=D9YBOYn10FAfeature=youtu.be

Sion Bird:
http://www.youtube.com/watch?v=M0MYNAN98alfeature=youtu.be

The Emaciated Mzungu Memorial Trench

Today it is raining, for the first time since my return. (Was that really three weeks ago?)

"That's not rain", a Tanzanian Crocodile Dundee would say, "This is rain!", unleashing from behind his back a vast torrent, whence river and road became indistinguishable. Twice a year in Tanzania, the oceans and lakes and jet stream and sun get together, and for a few months fill the skies with surprised rivers, which had expected to be more terrestrial. They very quickly establish their fluvial rights, however, and pour down to earth, rushing in every direction in search of their familiar banks.

In the process, they make something of a mess of the roads. Months of sun will have hard-baked the dirt roads, but also fractured them. Then stones below the surface get dislodged by over-burdened traffic, and the fissures get wider. The more traffic on the road, the more the need for its integrity but, ironically, the more the crunching and the cracking. Thereafter comes the rain, and the grateful river of water surges down the rifts, dislodges future silt and leaves behind swirling furrows crossing the roads this way and that. During the rain, the dirt roads are all-but impassable, but when the sun comes out, it serves to dry the furrows into ruts and bumps that challenge even Land Rover suspension – and there aren't many Land Rovers.

The front drive leading to our mission house was a case in point. The house (as you will by now have seen on YouTube) is tolerably comfortable, and the sitting room looks out over the steep valley to the hills beyond.

Many times I have sat on the veranda, gazing emptily towards the dry riverbed far below, wondering what to say in the next literary outpouring, but distracted by tantalising thoughts of distant sausages. It is a beautiful valley but, as a result of its steepness, the rain leaves the front drive less a road and more an assault course. The drive being circular, the rain cannot simply run down it, and so reluctantly hacks it into furrows, as it charges down the hill towards a tumultuous reunion on the valley floor.

Water, however, despite its destructive capacities, is very biddable. It only turns your front drive into a ploughed field because it is trying to get out of the way, and if you give it the option of getting out of the way more easily, it readily accepts taming. Thus the Emaciated Mzungu Memorial Trench.

The story went like this: more than a month into my stay in Berega, I was a wizened, puny vestige of my former self, with no opportunity to exercise (other than lifting an occasional heavy pan of inedible yellow things in order to discard them on the compost heap). On our visit to Dodoma, however, I saw a pick-mattock for sale, and pounced on it. A mattock is a beast of an instrument. Where a hobbit would use a hoe, a cave troll would use a mattock. It goes without saying, of course, that a pick-mattock is better for trench-building than a grubbing-mattock, because the pick-end enables removal of bigger rocks, while the mattock-end can hack out a trench, oblivious of roots and rubble. The entire tool, with handle, weighs about 12 kg. Having, with the pick, wheedled any stones out from the path of the mattock head, you then unleash the mattock onto Mother Earth, gashing a deep furrow in her flesh.

At the top of the drive, I planned the route that the water will take when the first rains arrive in November. Passers-by on the road stopped to admire the efforts of the emaciated *mzungu*, manfully standing up to the might of nature and pummelling the would-be trench into existence. Being out of condition, I had to rest after each blow. I would have rested half way through each, had it been an option. By the end of two hours, a few inches of trench were already demonstrating their proclivity, by directing a litre or so of *mzungu* sweat down the hill. From the boys of the village, flocking incredulously around, a polite murmur of what I took to be awed appreciation sniggered between them and the gathering mosquitoes.

The path of the trench I sketched out by two parallel lines running down the side of the drive, and onto the thirsty lawn below. The first half-metre, mattocked to perfection, is a veritable Suez. Sadly, however, I did not get much further with the trench before I left Berega, and Sion has now taken over. As a result of his blow-by-blow assault on the un-mattocked section, an Emaciated Mzungu Memorial Trench is now being grooved into the erstwhile random surface of Africa.

It will be completed. We know what we want, we know where we want it and we have begun. When the rain begins to fall, it may be that we will need to take account of the way water naturally flows, but thereafter it will flow with a sense of purpose, reinforcing the trench more deeply with each downpour. As the perceptive will have noticed, I have just managed to ooze my way into a relevant metaphor. Although I am now back with my own tribe, the journey to safe childbirth for future mothers in Berega's territory has begun. Careful hands are now deepening the commitment and purpose and direction. Things may unfold differently to our plan, but perhaps not by much. There is no going back to the random inefficiency of the past. It will be completed.

Beautiful examples of the irreversibility are the inspiring activities of Kofia. Their thriving website is the hub of both fundraising and spreading of awareness, but I particularly love the fact that they have knitted nearly 500 hats for Berega babies – and arranged a means of getting them there. Part of the vision is that, once babies have been delivered safely (which involves staying warm), they will continue to thrive when they go back to the villages. We want to follow up women back in the remote parts, and help ensure that their babies grow into healthy children. Having a Kofia hat might become the hallmark of a new era of health for this generation of babies.

Meanwhile, various enthusiasts are being inspired by the idea of a combined assault of community development and a community-based maternal/child health programme in Mnafu. It will allow women with no current realistic access to healthcare to have their babies in safe settings, and to raise their children without the expectation that 10% will die. The plan will now be fleshed out, having decided that, in the first instance, the priorities are bespoke transport and a health facility at Mnafu. Economic growth and education will follow, in partnership with the development of systems for safe childbirth and healthy under-fives.

The Diocese of Worcester has completed a hugely successful sponsored climb of Mt Kilimanjaro, raising thousands of pounds. A dozen or so people, some of whom had suffered altitude sickness while training on the Malverns, nevertheless managed to conquer the mountain. It was salutary to note, when flying home, that the mountain top was nearer to the plane than it was to the plains. I would have paid thousands not to climb it, so utter congratulations to those who even tried. Meanwhile, I have been humbled and touched by the support of friends – thank you. We are poised to make a difference where it will really count.

Meanwhile, back in Berega, progress continues. Isaac Mgego, the hospital director, is mustering forces at that end, ready and eager to begin a new era. Last month we saw reliable electricity become ensconced at the hospital. This month, for the first time in its history, a blood bank opened. It sounds a small thing but, until now, if a woman were bleeding heavily after delivery, we would first have had to call in a relative or a compatible donor before we could give her blood. Truly life-saving.

By the way, talking of life-saving, those following the tortuous tale of my nutritional nadirs will be delighted to know that my life is no longer in danger. I have eaten more pork and leek and spicy Cumberland sausages than any man's gall bladder should decently have to deal with. My blood pressure and waist size are creeping up nicely, and the sentinels of my liver have sent out for reinforcements. Furthermore, my exercise tolerance is beginning to build, and my legs no longer look like articulated wooden spoons. Part of the de-wooden-spooning programme is country walking, and so it was that, on Tuesday, we went to the Peak District, and I once again immersed myself in the English countryside. In the evening, pleasantly aching from ten miles of Derbyshire tracks and trails, fields and villages, woods and rivers, steep slopes up, steep slopes down (and even some steep flat places), all leading to deep satisfaction of arriving back where we had started from, I sat in the garden of the Devonshire Arms, and got outside a home-made game pie and a pint of ale, watching a yellow wagtail hop around the stones of a fresh, lively English stream. I was very satisfied to be home.

The next day, the full English breakfast strengthened me for the shock of the bill. A night in an English inn costs more than a month's living costs in Berega. In fact I do seem to have overdone my response to the rediscovered capacity to spend money (which I was always quite good at). In Tanzanian terms, my income is like the spring rain flooding down across my life, washing this way and that in lavish exuberance. I suspect that my wife thinks I need mattocking.

Us versus Mother Nature

In the six weeks since I left Berega, two mothers have died in the hospital. One young woman developed eclampsia at 28 weeks of pregnancy. Pre-eclampsia (the stage before eclampsia), is a malignant type of high blood pressure, which eventually picks off the organs one by one. Once the brain begins to be targeted, convulsions set in, and the disease is now called eclampsia. Treatment to hold back the fits and blood pressure can provide a window of enough hours to deliver the baby, and then to get on with bringing back the mother.

The worst eclampsia cases often occur at a premature gestation and, in the UK, the obstetrician must weigh the whole situation in deciding the timing of delivery: here in the UK, delivering a baby at 28 weeks results in a 90% chance of it surviving. In Berega, the figure is zero. No-one will have time and emotional energy, however, to grieve the baby: the mum's life is the priority. Her brain, liver, kidneys, lungs, heart and blood have to be coaxed back to normality, in a part of the world where the nearest they get to intensive care is a blood pressure cuff that works, used by someone who knows what to do with the results. Even the intravenous fluids are home-spun and the 'giving sets' erratic. In rural Tanzania, many do not make it, and nor did this terrified woman or her baby.

Saving a woman's life once eclampsia has set in is like trying to prevent death from lion attack – it is only hard if you did not see it coming from a long way off. Eclampsia is usually preceded by weeks of symptom-free high blood pressure. This woman would have been fetching her water and cooking her *ugali* without ever being aware of the silent predator that stalked her, nor of the tragically few days she had left to live.

I paint the picture in all its poignancy, to highlight the harsh injustice of nature in the raw. The reason that Chagongwe and Mnafu and Maguha and Tunguli have 200 times greater maternal mortality than Estonia is not because the latter has an ITU in every village. They do, however, have proper drips and blood pressure cuffs and people who know what to do with them. And roads. And systems of transport thereon.

Typical Tanzanian road inland

Preventing death from eclampsia is as simple as a village health worker (VHW) doing regular blood pressure checks, and referring anyone whose BP is above a certain level. When I look back on my choice of career, this was a central influence: turning potential tragedy into joy by such easy means.

The other death was also deeply harrowing. The problem was the combination of obstructed labour and haemorrhage, which conjunction is a grim reaper of young women in rural Africa. Again, in the final stages, the solutions are often beyond the resources of a hospital like Berega, but earlier on, much can be done. Seeing the woman before the labour became obstructed would be a big advantage, and once more a VHW has a role in encouraging waiting at the 'waiting mothers' house in the hospital, when labour is approaching. This would especially apply to those for whom a troublesome labour might be anticipated – for instance a slim 16-year-old in her first pregnancy. Better still is for her not to get pregnant – but where does an uneducated village girl even get the knowledge about contraception, far less the methods. Once more, VHWs can provide simple solutions.

It was a great joy, then, to help steer Berega's community development plan for mothers and children to its next stages. This began with triple and quadruple checking with the hierarchy at the hospital and their advisors that we have indeed captured their own vision, and that this is not something being done to them. Their response has been an overwhelming and heartfelt supplication that we might continue to make progress together towards the vision that they themselves set (by candlelight in evening meetings in the mission house, was it just two months ago?) The repetitive listening process is a powerful instrument for change: sometimes it is only on the fourth reading of what will become our catechism, that we spot the flaws and subtext and difficulties. The major changes made so far reflect the importance, not just of delivering babies safely, but of trying to prevent them becoming one of the countless under-fives that die in Berega's territory annually.

Success will depend on bringing together as many as have a part to play. Three of the key agencies at the UK end are the Diocese of Worcester, the charities Bread and Mission Morogoro. The latter two have as their entire *raison d'être* the development of Berega, although coming at it from different angles, different parts of the country and different funding sources. (Worcester Diocese has a wider brief of course, with the cure of the souls of half a million Worcestrians never something to be underestimated.) At the meeting, we shared our different takes on how we might help in the future – and there are as many different takes as there are different needs. Achieving focus, unity of purpose and division of labour is worth all the effort we will put into it. When obstacles inevitably arise, what controls our ability to remove them is not so much our power, as our combined determination.

Meanwhile, the charter of standards at Berega hospital is being translated into Swahili, with the intention of giving a copy to every member of staff. Given that this strategy has come from the hospital management with no external influence other than initial catalysis, they really mean business.

They need to. Tragedy still stalks and preys on the vulnerable. This week alone at Berega, there have been three major road traffic incidents, the biggest being 25 admissions in various states of brokenness. They all survived. When the rains come, it gets worse.

Of course, it is not only in rural Africa that such accidents occur, and readers will be devastated to know that I myself was unceremoniously unshipped from my bicycle on my first outing since my return. Coming down a hill towards a gate across the cycle path, my version is that I swerved to avoid a mother of quads and, in a feat of acrobatic heroism, flung myself and the bike into a paratrooper shoulder-roll when the most vulnerable of the quads went back to pick up her dolly. My fellow cyclists' version is that I was going too fast, and sailed over the handlebars like a flying frankfurter. Mother Earth eventually broke my fall by smashing my helmet into my head, in the process taking two inches off the length of my neck. Whichever version you care to believe, Mother Earth comes out of it as being hard and uncompromising. She needs us to take her in hand.

Allegri miserere

What is 31 minus 13? Answer: The Sixteen.

We went to see them in Coventry Cathedral on Wednesday. There are 31 in the squad for each away fixture, but they select just 16 – then throw in two extra sopranos to balance out the second basses, whose voices are richer and deeper than a subterranean Lindt chocolate lake. That leaves 13 on the bench and 18 on the pitch. Yet they call themselves The Sixteen. As there was no ref, they got away with it and at 7.30pm on the dot, they kicked off.

Unlike Sir Alex Ferguson, who seems to need the help of chewing what appears to be a squash ball in order for his players to obey his passionate gesticulations, (although I have to admit a grudging admiration for anyone who can, with a single get-those-chickens-off-the-road gesture, manage to tell the forwards to move ahead, and yet the goalie to stay where he is). Anyway, unlike him, the conductor of The Sixteen, Sir Harry Christophers, simply walked up to the hallowed Cathedral rostrum, neatly stuck his Wrigley's Spearmint between the Bishop's and the Archdeacon's, and began waving.

I said that there were 18 on the pitch, but 'on the pitch' does not begin to describe their precision, beauty and passion. I have been listening to (and singing) choral music since the 1960s (with breaks for eating sausages and delivering babies), and this was quite simply the best.

The starter was Palestrina, which at first sounded no more than beautiful. Then, walking up the aisles like mediaeval monks, and filling the vast cathedral with their dark, rich sound, echoing from nave, nook and niche, came what you suddenly realised were the missing men; chanting a deep, yearning, haunting, mediaeval plainsong. I felt all the awe of a feudal serf walking past York Minster at vespers on a soggy Martinmas Eve. It was all I could do not to die of pleasure and/or bubonic plague on the spot. The fog-horn, mastodon-low of the monks interlaced with the sparkling harmonies of the main group, like seams of praline in diamond (which, for the purists, cannot be a mixed metaphor, as it is a simile). You get the idea, anyway, that their singing was indescribably beautiful. But the best was yet to come.

The second piece was Allegri's Miserere. If you have never heard it, listen to it now – it is (or was, as I thought then), the most transcendently blissful piece of music ever written. So beautiful was it deemed in the past, that it was kept secret by the Vatican choir, and only sung once a year in the Sistine Chapel. Then Mozart heard it, wrote it down, and thereafter the souls of we ordinary citizens could immerse ourselves in it. The Sixteen's version, moving from the simplicity of the authentic article, to the modern embellished version, was indescribably sublime, but one feature in particular I wanted to mention.

When soldiers march across a bridge, they have to break the regular stomp-stomp of their relentlessly in-time boots, or else the bridge might begin to resonate at that frequency. Were it to do so, the continued stomping would feed an amplifying effect and, within a minute, the whole bridge could be undulating wildly, before spectacularly collapsing. If you are a squaddie on leave and want to try this, but are separated from your fellow stompers, the same effect can be achieved by moving a wet finger lightly round a crystal wineglass at a constant speed. What should be a tiny noise self-amplifies, until it is an all-pervading note, and finally the wineglass shatters in joy. Amplification of human voices, to make a sound which gradually expands until it fills and vibrates the building, can only be achieved if every one of the voices is perfectly blended with the next, every mouth-shape the same, every vocal nuance mastered to the same high degree and every pitch perfect. I have been in the same cathedral when 500 voices did not make as much sound as those 18 were capable of. The magic was that they could expand from a whisper to a cathedral-throbbing thrill in a heartbeat.

"Why", I hear you say, "is he drifting off on this musical odyssey?" "Aha!" I hear you answer yourself, oblivious to the seriousness of the potential psychiatric diagnoses typified by talking to yourself through someone else's book, "He is going to draw parallels between The Sixteen, and saving mothers and babies in rural Tanzania." Perhaps you are imagining that I would pick up on the idea that plainsong is all very beautiful, but that when it creatively harmonises with the efforts of others it fulfils itself. Or maybe you think I might point to the self-amplification that occurs when harmony is perfect, whence seemingly impossible effects can be achieved. Even the old structures can come tumbling down, under the persistent vibrancy of simple, resonant harmony, you may be thinking, I would note.

Certainly you would have a good point. Development in rural Tanzania is an echoing, clashing, plaintive emptiness, ready and waiting to be filled with the music of harmonised effort. Aligning the efforts of Berega hospital, the Diocese of Morogoro, the Tanzanian Health Agencies, Bread, Hands4Africa, Ammalife, Mission Morogoro, Kofia, the Diocese of Worcester and various universities, institutes, quangos and NGOs will be worth all the effort put in. Three key meetings are approaching, and a fair amount of email traffic. By Christmas, we will all be on the same sheet.

However, if you were expecting that I was going to be so predictable as to make such comparisons, you underestimate me. The actual story I was going to tell was this: Allegri Miserere was not the highlight of the show. After four centuries of prime time on Classic FM, move over Gregorio, and enter James Macmillan.

I had never been much of a fan of modern music. My unacceptably uncultured philosophy had been that, if you wanted to drop a piano from a tall building onto a barrel-organ player and his monkey; or if you wanted to put a tom-cat that keeps you awake at night in a food-blender with a duck-lure and some castanets; then by all means go ahead. But don't call it music. By my simplistic and uneducated take was this: if it sounded like you had made the wrong note, then the reason was likely to have been that you had made the wrong note. I knew that many modern composers were geniuses. I knew that they could have written like Tallis, but chose not to.

Benjamin Britten, for instance, was perhaps the archetypal 20th century genius. His tougher works, however, (unless you sang them as he planned, and that is quite an unlikely 'unless'), could have a tendency to sound like emptying a recycling bin onto the National Youth Orchestra when they were warming up. When I was in the Liverpool Philharmonic choir, 35 years ago, we sang Britten's War Requiem and a modern Russian piece 'Poem to October' on the same programme. We had no time to rehearse both well, so the conductor (looking at me, I think), told us: "Look! I don't mind if you sing the wrong notes, but when you do, for God's sake don't cover your face with your hands and then mouth the word 'Sorry'!" On the night, we pulled out the stops for the Britten, but the other we just winged. About three out of the 200 of us were on the right page when it finished, and some I think had already left the podium. We got a standing ovation. (The strange thing is I am not sure that the composer would have disapproved.)

Anyway, now the light has shone. Macmillan's modern Miserere was sublime, and even surpassed the genius of Allegri. It still had plainsong chanting. It still had blissful bursts of embellishment. It also at times expanded to fill the cathedral with thrilling perfection of resonance. But there was something new and bold and exhilarating that, once heard, could not leave you in the same state in which it found you.

So here is my point. A new music is happening in Africa. Something new and bold and exhilarating that, once heard, could not leave you in the same state in which it found you. Perhaps you might even want to be part of it?

Ammalife, hats and wandering nibs

My style to date has been to start on a thematic journey, meander seemingly unhinged-ly but then, with an attempt at an elegant literary double backflip with pike, deftly to return to base camp at the end.

This time, however, I do not think I have managed it.

This latest contribution to the chronicle turns out to be more of an A to B journey, of the sort that husbands make. (I say this fully aware of the dangers of gender stereotyping, and I would be more than happy to accept into the category of A-to-B-journeying-husbands, anyone of whatever chromosomal make-up, as long as they exhibit the trait. The husbandly trait is this: not only do they know the shortest way to the supermarket, avoiding traffic lights, pedestrian crossings and roundabouts, but they know it in metres, in minutes and in points of the compass, and would disembowel themselves, rather than look it up on GPS. On tougher journeys, they actually relish the challenge of getting there just as quickly, despite it being school drop-off time in the rush hour on the South Circular, with the home team playing a morning fixture, on the day that the National Union of Lumberjacks had injudiciously planned their traditional annual parade in memory of the Great Fire of London, at the same time and place that Greenpeace were lobbying Parliament on the deforestation of the inner cities. Furthermore, if achieving this on-time arrival involved off-road segments, river crossings, the Spanish Steps, or squeezing through a little-known defect in the wire fencing around a disused aerodrome, then so much the better. If this is you, and if you have been known to cut off all communication with your spouse for a week because s/he went through an unnecessary traffic light on the way home, then you are, of whatever gender, a husband.)

One of the main reasons for this husbandly directness is that I want to leap straight in and tell you about Ammalife (http://www.ammalife.org/), who have taken under their wing the Berega plans for saving the lives of mothers and children in the remote area of Mnafu. Ammalife, whose purpose is to make a difference to mothers throughout the world, is a rising star amongst such charities. Their founder trustee, Professor Arri Coomarasamy, is one of the top researchers in international women's health, and has collaborations in many countries, including Tanzania.

(I remember him, though, when he was a doe-eyed youth. He was my houseman/junior intern many moons ago, and perhaps he is the man he is today because I did not stint in using on him the well-honed tools of the day for nurturing intellectual growth: humiliation, bombastic overbearing outbursts and insistence on the punctilious use of outmoded and sometimes dangerous therapies.

"Coomarasamy! Why did you not lance these leeches before mixing them into the linseed-and-sparrow-liver poultice?"
"I am truly sorry sir, but it seemed as if her piles were already improving with the honey-and-hedgehog-skin gamgee.")

Anyway, Ammalife gets things done. They make a difference and, what's more, they put considerable effort, at no expense to the charity, in finding out what it is that does make a difference. With their high-profile partners, they apply for grants from international organisations to run large and well-constructed studies in under-resourced settings in many Asian and African countries, their most recent one published in The Lancet. Their interventions are often simple things. In a remote part of Pakistan, for instance, they have issued pregnant women who come to antenatal clinic with a taxi voucher. When the woman goes into labour, the voucher is presented and, when time might truly mean life or death, none of it is lost trying to find transport – nor money for transport. The cost to Ammalife is in pennies and the saving is in lives. It is not surprising then, that Arri Coomarasamy representing Ammalife has been asked to lead on one of the UK's main charity collaborations, to advise on sound intervention in maternal and child health.

There is a reason I am stressing Ammalife, and it is this. It is much more than a shot in the arm to have had the health care aspects of the Berega /Mnafu project housed within their organisation. They are not just being nice – they like what we are doing. They think it hits the spot. What is more, I will be reporting to them twice a year and drawing on their wisdom and, hopefully, critical friendship.

So look out on the Ammalife site for a page on our plans to make a difference in remote Tanzania.

Talking of making a difference, I have to share with you this photo:

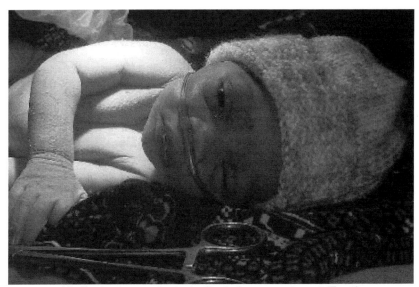

Kofia hat on a baby's first day on planet Earth

This was knitted by the worthy women of Guildford (the hat, not the baby). When Dr Blanché Oguti visited Berega this year, she was shocked to discover that vulnerable new-born babies cannot be adequately resuscitated if they are cold. Death and brain damage from this ironic cause in a tropical country are all too common, where newborn clothing is wet and thin. Blanché talked to her mentor, Dr Debbie Donovan. A few months later, the charity Kofia has already knitted 1,000 hats, and the picture you see is of the first ever use. The baby will keep the hat, and perhaps, one day, as we have already noted, these Kofias might be the hall mark of a looked-after childbirth – one where the woman and her baby have been cared for in the right place at the right time, by those who know what they are doing. Those hats, back in the village, will send a poignant message, from the privileged to the grateful.

I have much more to say, but will save myself until when all the meetings and first phase groundwork of the plans are complete. In particular, the charities Hands4Africa and Bread are going to be vital. Their frequent visits to Berega, to troubleshoot and to develop, have had progressive impact over the years: on primary schooling/education; the establishment of a nursing school; helping the hospital do its job; helping the community with transport, buildings and agronomy and more. When we are all completely clear as to who is doing what, where and when, we will then be ready to sign off a collaborative plan for stepping boldly into Mnafu, to begin walking with them on their journey into the 21st century.

Each step must be solid, and each step will take us further from the numb toughness of the past. It's really happening.

Well, I am coming to the end of this chapter, and seem to have taken you from Ammalife to Bread (via Kofia and H4A) in a fairly logical sequence. A to B, like a husband. I feel a little awkward about this, especially towards those who might have expected something a little more James Joycey. Indeed, it was in deference to such fans of the wandering nib, that my style to date has been to start on a thematic journey, meander seemingly unhinged-ly, but then, with an attempt at an elegant literary double backflip with pike, deftly to return to base camp at the end.

This time, however, I do not think I have managed it.

An ebb tide

"A rising tide lifts all the boats". A cheerily positive proverb, with something of an undiscerning optimism. Unseen and unintended benefits accrue when a big enough boost is given to the system.

I had been glibly thinking that my visit to Berega might have been something of a rising tide. Plenty of improvements occurred, many unlooked for. I had never expected, for instance, to see a charter of standards emerge, nor a 30-minute maximum delay for Caesareans, nor a plan for collaborative community development, nor a wonderful hat-knitting frenzy causing fleeces to be topping the futures market in Wall Street. Besides the unexpected benefits, there were the expected ones: the AMOs got better at Caesareans; the midwives got better at resuscitating babies; and the Tim Henman of the culinary arts got better at soaking stony-hard yellow things mixed with grit overnight before creating *intestins douloureux de ragoût de haricots jaunes* – best served with anything edible.

The 'rising tide' axiom has something of a disquieting history, however. It was first used by a Roman Republican politician to reassure the Senate that the vast sum he was suggesting that they sink into a water project, on land coincidentally owned by his family's associates, would produce ripples of benefit spreading out across the country. Maggie Thatcher, the Iron Lady, later made the philosophy her own. (I may have misunderstood this next thought slightly, coming, as I do, from a somewhat biased and antipathetic position towards the greedier of the multinationals.) Anyway she believed that if you made extremely rich people inexpressibly more wealthy, then they would spend some of the extra money on buying more peasants. (Please let me know if I haven't quite captured the soul of monetarism there.)

What none of us realised, as Maggie lifted our boats above the muddy banks of inflation, was that tides turn. A rising tide is followed by an ebb tide. (The moon, it turns out, is the culprit. It bestows its silver seemingly unstintingly, but all the time has been trying to steal our water. Hats off to Isaac Newton, by the way. What sort of brain do you have to have which, when awoken abruptly from a summer slumber by an apple on the head, unleashes the following train of thought:

What attracted that apple to my head?

It was surely my head itself?
What if my head attracts all things, not just solids, but liquids too?
Let me check it out with this glass of beer…
Gadzooks! It is true!
But the man in the moon's head is immeasurably bigger than mine…
What if he is trying to drink our seas? … etc)

A rising tide does indeed lift all the boats, and gives each a few precious hours of possibility. Each newly invigorated boat needs a crew, and a purpose and seaworthiness, if it is not to be found later floundering on the rocks. Choose which of the boats are most important to you and, when the tide goes out, let them be ready. Unfortunately for five women of Berega and its surrounding villages, if my visit was a rising tide, then its ebb has left their families and children mourning the loss of a mother, a wife, a daughter. Five mothers have died in childbirth since I came back nearly three months ago, and it is difficult to know which of their stories was the most harrowing. I think probably Mpendwa's story troubled me most, and it has left the hospital in shock. Mpendwa lived in a village 40 kilometres from the hospital and, with the November rains on the way, she chose to come and stay in the 'waiting mothers' house, rather than risk being left in obstructed labour on the wrong side of a torrent. So she waited with the other mothers and the relatives – plaiting hair in the afternoon sun after finishing the fetching and fire-lighting and carrying and washing and cooking and cleaning. Giggles and girlish gossip, while trying not to think too much about the family left at home to fend for themselves until she returned with the new baby.

Obstructed labour was what indeed happened. After a month of patient waiting, Mpendwa went into labour, made no progress and was taken for the Caesarean that should have saved her life. The baby came out and cried lustily. Then suddenly came a rare complication of the anaesthetic, and the team, with their primeval equipment and under-developed responsiveness to crises did too little, too late. Her heart stopped beating. She never saw her baby.

The reason that this was the most heart-rending of the five deaths was the effect that such a death has on the other mothers. No-one will look on Mpendwa's death as being what anyway would have happened had she stayed at home. She would indeed have died at home, just as one or two do every week in Berega's territory. But she came, for a month, to the place, the haven, where we all hope that women might expect life and health. Despite the fact that every successful Caesarean at Berega means two lives saved, and that the huge majority of women do indeed survive the Caesarean, the death of Mpendwa sent out the message: "Here be danger! Stay at home!"

And stay at home is exactly what one other young mother did. She could see the hospital perimeter fence from the hut in which the traditional birth attendant struggled to stop the bleeding after her childbirth. By degrees, she gradually realised that her life was ebbing away, and that she must say goodbye to the child that would never know her. By the time she arrived at the hospital gates, she was minutes from death, and heroic effort could not save her.

Three other deaths; three other tragic tales.

By contrast, when another rising tide washed up Berega's inlets, many lives were saved. Grace Parr, a Canadian resident, was perplexed on her first day of a volunteer stint in Africa, to find a relatively empty maternity ward. She needn't have worried. Each of the next seven days brought a new eclamptic patient – having seizures due to high blood pressure. Untreated, the condition is fatal for mother and baby. Grace stayed by many a bed that week, nurturing and nursing, and all seven mothers and five of their babies went home healthy.

Meanwhile, Sion Williams has now worked tirelessly for six months with barely a day off, for no pay, and countless families have had their loved ones returned to them intact. His love sends out an even more powerful message than his medicine. David Curnock, a retired paediatrician from England, goes out annually for two months with his wife Anne, and each visit finds a few more boats afloat.

What can we learn, then? Berega, and the quarter of a million population in its remote mountain villages, need a rising tide. Not just a trickle, but a tide, and one which to last long enough to train the crew, to clarify the purpose, to make the boats seaworthy.

Then the ebb tide becomes just another opportunity.

Grandma's Juice

Words. In this book, I use them to depict the dire reality of life in a remote part of Africa. But the tragedy unfolds there, whether or not I describe it. (Just like when I am sent to do the shopping: what I buy is going to be wrong, whether or not my wife gets the chance later to give me personal feedback. What's the difference anyway between fresh crème and crème fraiche? A trifle, surely?)

Anyway, it is the reality that matters. The words can get in the way. The situation in Berega (as in many other parts of the world) is bursting with meaning and import and consequence, but all you get are words. My words, in the case of Berega. Can they be enough?

My 21-month grandson, already a master of the inadequacy of words, illustrates the point: "Man-ma's juice is hot!" "Man-ma's juice" was my cup of tea. This was Freddie's first full sentence, at the start of that wonderful decade between not being able to speak, and not wanting to. It was so cute that we have not had the heart yet to begin the rigid programming of mind which the World demands of its inmates.

The sentence was nevertheless wrong in every way: he calls both my wife and me 'Man-ma', a corruption of 'Grandma', but I am in fact 'Dandad'. It was not juice, it was tea. And although he was correct to infer that beverages made with boiling water can indeed be hot, this particular cupful was at best tepid. The nub is this: did we pull him up on the inadequacy of his descriptive powers? ("You foolish child! I am your male antecedent; a beverage by definition cannot be a vegetal extract; and this specific cup was barely above the melting point of caesium at atmospheric pressure!) Yes, we did.

No, not really. Instead, we boasted about the cleverness and cuteness of little Freddie to all those who have not yet got into the habit of crossing to the other side of the road when they see us coming with a smug look on our faces, and a finger fumbling for the photo album on the phone.

Freddie also deploys many other teddy-cuddling cutenesses. My favourite is his tendency to use 'No' to mean both 'no' and 'yes':

("You poor little baby, you are so hungry. Do you want some food?"

"Nooo-oooo-sob sob sob-ooooo."
"Here it is then…")

(By the way, these verbal *faux pas* are presumably designed by nature to endear us to what are otherwise machines for turning anything edible into poo. "I'm weally, weally hungwy" is far more likely to induce a beleaguered parent to stump up a sausage than: "Mother, the hour of my repast has surely slipped into the abyss of forgotten dreams. Ah! The sweet sound of sausages, that breathes upon a bank of bacon, stealing, and giving odour!" Without the endearing mistakes, they weally would be hungwy. Perhaps the highly intelligent Cro-Magnon man died out because their children's first sentences were particularly annoying – "Oi! Pig-face! Get me grub! Now!")

The nub is this: words are important, but alone are not enough. Freddie, like rural Tanzania, is bursting with meaning and import and consequence, for instance about the potential danger of Grandma's juice or bad roads or high blood pressure. The expression of this does not do justice to the reality or the understanding.

This last month has been full of similar inadequacy of expression. My time has been split between getting harmony and getting money. The various charities working for Berega's future need to harmonise, and that means having a collective plan that says clearly what we are all trying to do, how and by when.

Meanwhile, grant applications demand a certain practised style in the use of words. I find myself writing: 'The evidence-based intervention propounds a setting-specific self-sufficient synergy between the inter-agency evaluative action objectives and the … er … chickens'. (Often I run out of steam towards the end of these sentences, which is why I am not a very successful grant-raker.)

Words, words, words, but what of the mum who does not return home to her children? Does '1% maternal mortality per childbirth' convey enough of the sadness? Does it capture the empty, desolate weariness of the six- and eight-year-old sisters as they struggle next day to find water and carry it home? All hope of schooling now lost, how will they survive?

I feel the inadequacy, then, as well as the usefulness, of having adopted a catchy title for what we are trying to do: 'Embrace' – Empowering Women to Receive Adequate Care and Equality'. We now also have a logo, a flyer, a standing order form, a Facebook page and a Twitter account. Thanks to Ammalife, we have a Mother charity and, thanks to Debbie and Blanché, a global following amongst the world's pearly queens. Thanks to lots of friends, we have some money. Thanks to Bread, Hands4Africa, Mission Morogoro, Isaac, Abdallah, the Diocese of Worcester and others, we have a plan.

What is needed now is somehow to convey what is really happening there and how it is changing. What goes right, what goes wrong. What helps, what hinders. Which sentiment, softly spoken by the right person to the right person, will have the power to stimulate a new understanding and a new expectation in this beautiful and untouched part of Africa.

Words will not be enough.

The Samson Dilemma (the limited power of baldness)

This month I met a wonderful and impressive couple: Dr Ahmed Ali and his wife Elizabeth. Ahmed is on his way to Berega for a two-month stint as obstetrician in residence – the first of what we hope will be many journeys. On the next visit, Elizabeth also hopes to go, and her midwifery talents will be greatly valued. Inspiringly, they have chosen to close the door on very successful UK careers, and to spend the next phase of their lives making a difference where it is sorely needed.

(When I was young, I might have referred to this as the 'twilight' of their careers. However, now that I am not just at twilight but hurtling towards the setting of Venus in Capricorn, this couple's careers seem positively early afternoon by comparison.)

Of course when we met, Ahmed's mind was full of the last-minute preparations. These are all the more important when the trappings of developed-world comfort and convenience are not likely to be available in the place to which you are headed. For instance, this is what a shopping mall looks like in Berega:

Berega shopping mall

It would be fine for buying sacksful of the more indigestible parts of the faba bean plant, but expect a puzzled silence if you ask for a cappuccino-frother-plug-in for your iPad.

When going through the list of things to ensure to take (phone; charger; Kindle; iPad; Sanatogen, etc), it transpired that Ahmed (in his words), needed to "join to the present to go to the past". He had, it seems, been living in the late 20th century, when books were made of paper, phones were designed for speaking to people, and GPS was a Gammon and Pineapple Sandwich. Suddenly, he now had to equip himself with the electronic accoutrements of today, in order to spend a couple of months in what, for most of the rural Tanzanian population (for health purposes at least), is the 18th century. Ironic.

When I think of it, though, I am not so sure that the analogy is a perfect one. They had blankets in the 18th century, but Berega has no blankets, nor good food, nor comfortable beds. Equally, 300 years ago, they had no anti-malarials, no vaccines and no antibiotics; but the presence of these modern miracles in Berega has not compensated for the dismal conditions in which many children are raised. With an under-five mortality of 10%, and maternal mortality approaching 1%, Berega's territory has not moved on far from Walpole's England. In the villages, the reason is clear: little has happened in the intervening three centuries to make a difference.

In the hospital itself, however, we might have hoped for better. Meagrely equipped though it is, it should nevertheless be ready deal at least tolerably well with the majority of life-threatening situations for mothers and their children.

In the past, to be honest however, clinical standards have been simply too unresponsive to the many fillips that they have received. (Thus my reluctance to kick off the first year of 'Embrace' until we are sure that we will be bringing women into somewhere safe and effective.) However, with the arrival of Ahmed, a new champion, hopes are high. This is particularly so, as he is in fact the latest in a whole bunch of champions. (Champions, it seems, are like buses – you wait ages for one, and then three come at once (or, in Mexico, a magnificent seven).

There are some interesting parallels, by the way, between the burgeoning help in Berega and the Magnificent Seven. The most obvious is that both Yul Brynner and I prefer to leave our scalps open to the fresh air, rather than choking them with cultivated keratin. Both of us recognise, however, that baldness alone cannot help save a village. And for all the immense efforts of Isaac, Stanley, Abdallah, Sion, Brad/Hands4Africa, John, Tony and the Diocese of Worcester/ Mission Morogoro, Gary, David, Mike and the amazing worthies of Bread, my good self and others too many to mention, the hospital has still been struggling in many ways, not least in relation to clinical standards. Nevertheless, each year the lives of many are saved – lives which, without relentless hard work, would have been lost. Eclampsia and haemorrhage and malaria and malnutrition and the rest of their deadly crew still regularly raid and kill. They are mainly fought off, but more could be done to deter these bandits.

Now, suddenly, opportunistically, the Magnificent Seven effect is beginning to kick in. (You may know that the story was based on a 16th century Japanese samurai myth. The idea, however, is as old as story-telling itself: that, from an extremely beleaguered position, some fickle-finger-of-fate-ing leads to a burgeoning wave of powerful help, and the baddies are vanquished. I, for one, believe that the finger of fate is not in fact that fickle, and that the extraordinary constellation of heroes gathering around to help, is not here by chance alone.)

Nevertheless, it is about as unlikely a story as ever inspired Hollywood. Even I do not know the full details. (For instance, I genuinely don't remember how I got involved with Berega. I remember making the vaguest of enquiries in response to an ad about a short spell in Ethiopia. The next thing I remember is buying peanut butter in Dar es Salaam.) Anyway, to cut a long, long story short, a year ago, Sion was headed for a job with Médecins Sans Frontières. By a hugely unlikely life-upheaving coincidence, four months later, he had begun a year's job at Berega. A veritable Steve McQueen of the stethoscope, he began knocking off baddies on every side. Then came myself, Dan, Marjaan, Blanché and the recurrent hero, David Curnock.

More recently, Ann Kang, who works in the hotel industry, met Sion in a random bar in Zanzibar. Utterly incredibly, shortly afterwards she had begun a three-month stint working in Berega. Her legacy includes, not only the first ever monitoring of clinical standards, (accomplished with the new assistant matron), and too many other works to name, but also the gathering of tens of thousands of dollars to sponsor village children through education – the single-most determinant of health in the world.

Check out her amazing story at
http://www.anninberega.blogspot.co.uk/

And Sion's at: http://doctorwoctor.blogspot.co.uk/

The story keeps on expanding. The medical establishment had recently been up to three: Olivia Vandecasteele a Belgian tropical medicine expert, and Sander Wever, a Dutch head of an emergency department, found themselves drawn into the whirlwind. What a difference to have these experienced professionals dedicating themselves to the cause.

Most extraordinary of all has been the expansion of Kofia. From the modest hope to knit 50 hats to send a message of love from Guildford to Tanzania via Basingstoke, Blanché Oguti and Debbie Donovan's efforts have blossomed to an impossible extent, where many people in many countries are now knitting for Africa. With the arrival of the wonderful Nina Oakman offering herself as Kofia's link in Dar, they are set to begin helping poor women throughout Tanzania to tackle the deadly problem of neonatal hypothermia. (By the way, although sending knitting across the world sounds a little old-fashioned, and although it may seem wiser simply to send money and commission some local wool-taming, success is not measured only in financial value. Thousands of people are finding, not just purpose, but an outlet for their generosity and goodwill towards the plight of the needy. Kofia hats, blankets and clothes are a symbol of an increasing readiness to share responsibility in this small world which we cohabit.)

When I was about 40, my scalp hair began falling out and, like Samson and Yul Brynner, I was quite upset about it. In Samson's case, his hair was his power, so getting a number 2 all over was more than inconvenient. When I was 40, I also was struck by the limited power of baldness.

Little did I realise then that the power also flows through teachers' chalk, random drinks in Zanzibar, and woollen hats.

A Bridge Too Far

As you know, this book narrates the story of an attempt to help save the lives of mothers and babies in rural Tanzania. The problem is that the more story there is to tell, the less chance I seem to get to tell it. In the midst of responding to an expanding network of inspiring, encouraging and well-grounded support, sometimes getting round to narrating the next chapter at the end of a day's g-mailing can turn out to be a bridge too far.

('G-mailing', by the way, for future generations who read this book after finding a copy of it saved on an electronic papyrus clutched to my chest within my sarcophagus, along with money to pay the boatman and some cheese-and-pickle sandwiches to avoid the lunch queues on the other side, was not, as you might have thought, the process of sending mail at exactly the speed of sound. It was in fact a device used in the early 21st century for enabling you to get through more correspondence on the slow train to Euston via Milton Keynes, than either Milton or Keynes managed in their lifetime.)

Anyway, today the g-mailing is taking a back seat while I attempt a bookish bonanza, to help bridge the communication gap between our wildly varying existences on this increasingly small planet.

Talking of bridges, one of the (barely credible) stories awaiting narrating is the collapse of the Berega bridge, (Google Earth 6°11'20.21" S 37° 8'28.26" E) in a flash-flood on the Mgugu river on January 21. The rainfall in Berega itself was only average for the time of year. Far upstream, however, a circle of mountains gathered up the angry waters like Rawhide heading up a herd of feisty steers, and unleashed them on the unsuspecting foothills below. The torrent swept away 11 railway stations, two major bridges and countless homes and crops. It would have swept away more transport infrastructure, but Tanzania has not got any. The river bed is, of course, impassable for all but the bravest, and so more than 100,000 sq km of territory is now cut off. To lose your food supply at the same time as losing the potential to replace it is especially worrying for many villagers.

Berega bridge, before and after

Maybe, however, some unexpected good will come from the turmoil. The President of Tanzania has already visited Berega's ex-bridge, and apparently a contract has now been signed with an international engineering company to build a new one. Furthermore, the whole episode has raised national awareness of the abysmal transport systems. As a result, President Kikwete recently met England's Nick Clegg, and asked for the UK to donate some old locomotives to populate Tanzania's railway. The Thin Controller responded with a commitment of sorts, which of course is as good as money in the bank, (or in this case, rolling stock on the tracks).

And it is painfully needed: last year, due to dilapidation, Tanzanian rail managed to transport only 2% of the anticipated shipments. Even had it managed the entire lot, its meagre 4,000 km of railway (in a country with 5,185 km of borders and coastline) would have left many of the loads woefully distant from their destination. This is a bit like saying: "So you want some goods shipped from Paris to Prague? No problem. Just drop them off at Marseilles, and we will take them all the way to Venice, where you can pick them up, except if they happen to be part of the 98% of shipments for which Venice was a bridge too far, in which case you can pick them up from Marseilles. Alternatively, and this is only a suggestion, leave them in Paris, and then at least you will know where they are."

It is not surprising, then, that the majority of haulage in Tanzania is performed on the roads. There are about a dozen inter-city roads in Tanzania – one main crossroads every few hundred kilometres. There are almost no dual carriageways. 'Duel carriageways', on the other hand, are far too common: this happens when your eye was momentarily diverted from the road by a Maasai warrior on his mobile phone, perhaps buying a lion-trap on eBay, and you suddenly realise that two trucks are hurtling towards you, playing chicken. A chicken, ironically (well a thin one, anyway), would have survived the encounter, as plenty of Tanzanian highways are sensibly of two-truck-and-a-fat-chicken width. But not two-truck-and-your-chosen-means-of-conveyance. It is rare to do the Dar to Morogoro run without seeing at least three cars in a ditch.

The other death-seeking road-occupant is the ubiquitous minibus. More than half of Tanzania's vehicles are some sort of bus or coach. There are no timetables – the first one to come takes the passengers, and the first one to get to the destination gets the prime pick-up for the homeward run. It will not amaze you to learn, then, that, despite having

50 times fewer motor vehicles on the road per capita compared to the UK, Tanzania has seven times the fatality rate. The moral is: only travel with a seasoned Buddhist monk driver, in a strong car, with a whale song tape creating a sense of *bien-être* to keep you calm in a crisis – and look both ways before crossing a bridge.

Of course, the majority of river crossings are too far from the main road to need to worry about trucks and minibuses. The main form of transport on the dirt roads is the motorbike, and in every village someone will be selling pints of fuel in old Coke bottles stacked up on a makeshift counter by the roadside, getting worryingly hot in the sun. When motorbikes are the only transport bar ox cart, then if you came out without your oxen, you have little option.

The motorbike is indeed the principal way that a woman in need would access the hospital, but ironically those most in need are those furthest from the hospital, and usually the poorest. An average fare from a village 40 or 50 kilometres and three rivers away might be 10,000 Tanzanian shillings – £4. Not much to you or me, but the price might double in a night-time emergency, and a little extra is added for the sister or mother sitting second pillion. Her role is to oversee safe arrival, to give blood and make food and, for the unfortunate, to take home the body. The final price of a single ride might be as much as £10 – a week's wages for most – and even then, in the rainy season, they have to hope that the roads and rivers will be passable. For these reasons, many women in the more remote areas simply leave it too late, hoping that the bleeding will stop or that the baby will eventually come. When finally they realise that they will die without help, they collect the fare from friends and relatives, say a poignant goodbye to the children and set off to cross the most important bridges of their life, hoping that none of them will be too far.

The project Embrace will aim to save these lives, and is about to take its first steps – the mapping of the roads to Tunguli and Mnafu and beyond. We need to know that we are going to the right places, and we need to be able to measure what we are doing: are we indeed making things better? Are women-in-need really coming in to hospital and going home with healthy babies? When we know the names of the villages, we can begin to check routinely the hospital records, as to whether and how the women from each community arrive. And so we begin with a driver, a camera and a GPS machine. Every mile or two he stops: who lives here? What are the names of the villages? How many mothers of under-fives? Where do they deliver their babies? The results are entered both on Google Earth and on living maps. It is surreal that, 160 years after David Livingstone, we are treading laboriously in his footsteps to produce the first-ever accurate map. When we have finished the mapping, we might hope that Embrace will be ready to begin.

The project is now taking more detailed shape, under the influence of many good minds, and if you want to see what can be achieved by this type of approach in remote and isolated parts of Africa, check out this heart-warming video:

http://vimeo.com/12427420

If Embrace can achieve the same seismic shifts in attitude and culture, it will be the start of a new era of hope for many women. A pre-requisite, however, is the maintenance of high standards at Berega Hospital, where key new players are beginning to make their presence felt in many important ways. Many others are helping shape the vision – Ammalife, Mission Morogoro, Bread, Hands4Africa, Diocese of Worcester, Kofia, as well as others not yet connected, who are planning visits to Berega in the year ahead. Exciting times. I hope that they will find the river crossable by then and the waters tamed.

It is thought-provoking that the substance of which Tanzanian health, economy and agriculture is in most need, is the very one whose excess destroys all three.

An interesting speculation arises with regard to our own extraordinarily persistent and widespread excess water problems in the south and west of England, and especially in the Somerset Levels, or the 'Bristol Channel' as it is now known. (It's the West Country's answer to Holland, but without the dykes.) Is it any consolation to an erstwhile affluent Somerset Leveller, I wonder, that someone else has got it worse? As she wades waist-deep from her lounge to her kitchen, clad in her pink Versace fisherman's wellies to make an ironic water-based infusion, is she sparing a thought for the flood-swept river beds of rural Tanzania? As she unhitches her occasional-table raft from the door lintel, to make the whitewater dash to her dentist in Bath to get her bridge replaced, well aware of the pirate menace that infests the quieter sections of the A367, is she counting her blessings?

I guess that people do not really appreciate what they have. What they truly do appreciate is the lack of sudden change to what they have (or rather they would do, if it were not the case that such appreciation is often retrospective). Interestingly, this even seems to apply when the sudden change is apparently for the good – winning the lottery is necessarily more tumultuous than not doing so, and by no means guarantees a happier existence. (I have even thought about setting up an alternative 'Zen Lotto', in which the top prize is free entry to the following week's Lotto.)

I guess that my most tumultuous sudden change in recent years was my two months in the sausage-and-malbec-deprivation chamber of Africa. A little before that, I had been happily scribbling away my retirement, vaguely aware of a niggling and nudging in my conscience that maybe I still had a Caesar or two left in me. Then suddenly I am doing them. One moment I am living a heady life, pork-and-leeking at will, and washing down the day with Argentina's plummiest. A flash of Kismet's prestidigitation, and I am saving lives in a forgotten corner of a different century. It happened too quickly for me to object. Had I been rational, perhaps I might have been put off by the absurdity of the ambition: to build a bridge to women living in a mediaeval African culture in mud-hut villages 5,000 miles away. I might have thought, and so might you, that this was too far-flung to reach, too far-reaching to meddle with, too far-fetched to countenance, and too far-ranging to bridge.

Too far? No.

Woman Power

The answer is 1metre 80 cm (5 ft 11 inches). This titbit of knowledge is so surprising (nearly six feet!) that to call it 'trivia' is demeaning.

The question to which this is the answer is, of course: how tall was 'Mary, Queen of Scots?' Mary Queen of Scots was the grand-niece of King Henry VIII. She was Queen of Scotland from infancy, was Queen of France *un peu* and was mother of King James I of England. She was taller and better educated than just about anyone on the planet in the 16th century, and possessed compassionate beliefs and sparkling social skills. And yet she never had power. She was made use of by her men; spent half her adult life imprisoned; never saw her son again after his last breastfeed; and, finally, was beheaded when they could not think of anything other use for her.

You do not need to be much of a feminist to feel that she had been somewhat simon-cowelled. (Cockney rhyming slang for 'disembowelled' – itself a metaphor for humiliation of the vulnerable by a dental flosser. More Cockney rhyming.)

Before I became an obstetrician, I was an alpha male rugby-playing surgeon and, rejecting the stereotype, never thought of myself as much of a feminist. Indeed, despite living then in a world of burgeoning gender equality, I am ashamed to say that, in my ignorance, I vaguely thought of feminists as women who wanted to be like men. It was only when I came to a deeper maturity that I realised that no insult could be more below-the-belt. Why would a woman want to be like a man? Of course, not all men historically were bombastic, insensitive, dominant, aggressive, grumpy, sex-mad, power-crazed odd-job men, but as a gender, over the millennia, we have indeed done our share of sulking angrily at the lack of sexual responsiveness of a vulnerable and abused woman, whilst putting up a shelf. True, many of us were good for fighting off lions, intruders and money spiders, but I have to accept the argument that this might not have been sufficient recompense for childbirth, home-building and disempowerment.

Fortunately, here in the UK, we have mainly left behind the epochs of gender stereotypes, in theory at least, and my wife these days expects me to share in the cooking, just as I expect her to help in the turning-on of the computer to try to fix the black-screen problem.

However, this balmy concord in the division of household chores nevertheless remains the exception rather than the rule in many parts of the world, and in particular in rural Africa. In the recent past, men were the workers and before that the warriors, and roles were tough on all sides. So much has changed that it is now impossible to make sweeping generalisations. Yet it remains a grim fact that many women are born to a life (and death) of recurrent childbirth, bereavement, toil and exhaustion. This is not necessarily because men choose that it should be so, but rather this is the way that it always was. In the sleepy heat of the African sun, somehow things never get round to being different. It is accepted.

What has proven most effective in changing this, in developing countries on every continent, is the empowerment and education of women. Once women start meeting in groups with the purpose of discussing their difficulties, and once this process has the blessing and cooperation of the men (which it often does), then suddenly barriers which had seemed insuperable to the individual melt like glaciers in Surrey. (A strange simile, I hear you say, but do you see any glaciers in Surrey?) Solutions emerge. An interesting characteristic of solutions, by the way, is that they don't have to be right. They just have to be tried, and the process leads you another step ahead. Suddenly people are asking why they should have six children; why they should not have cleaner water, nearer by; why they cannot create employment; why bare subsistence should be the norm; why their children cannot go to school; why they should be so susceptible to ill health; and why they have to die to bring life into the world.

After many iterations, the project Embrace (Empowering Women and Babies to Receive Adequate Care and Equality), has now defined exactly how it plans to tackle the complex and interwoven problems underpinning death of mothers and babies, and it has taken its first baby steps.

The planning of an intervention to be 'done to' a community is fraught with difficulty and, ultimately, is likely to founder in the Mire of Unseen Difficulties. This has been the troubled history of African development: "When you do what you always did, you get what you always got." On the other hand, when communities have only hope, rather than expectation that anything should ever be better, how do you get them to want the interventions you have up your sleeve?

As we have already noted, women's groups have provided the answer.

It was with great pleasure then that I have been receiving the emails from Elizabeth Ali, and Drs Sion, Ahmed and Abdallah about progress that has been made. Two points need highlighting in particular. The first is that Sion and Abdallah met to finalise the methodology that Embrace will be using. They have discovered that a village infrastructure exists which can be tapped into and harnessed for whatever development needs are being addressed. We had no idea that this infrastructure of hamlet leaders, village health workers and traditional birth attendants was already formed, but relatively dormant in every community. It gives us a powerful way in, for the formation of women's groups. Once the touch paper has been lit, we then hope to muster, direct and coordinate support, so that issue by issue the communities can begin to tackle their pressing problems. Here is a distillate of Sion's vision:

"We must first identify areas with problems – so far this includes Berega, Tunguli and Mnafu. This requires the mapping. Next we meet with four key groups of people – TBAs, village health workers, hamlet leaders and village leaders, to get them on board.

"We will ask these community leaders to identify appropriate women, to become key people in the running of the groups at hamlet level.

"The purpose of these groups is, first, to identify problems, which will then inform the next stage of the project- getting people to deliver in a good, safe hospital."

The second breakthrough has been in the mapping. It turns out that the hamlet leaders already know much of the information that we need. This means that we can simply go to each hamlet, meet the key people, explain what we are trying to do (with cautions about raising expectations too quickly) and then measure GPS coordinates. (Look at me, using terms like 'GPS' as if I had been raised on Google Earth. If the truth be known, until last September I had thought it meant, not gammon and pineapple, but Gherkin and Pastrami Sandwich, and I had always puzzled how New Yorkers used bread products to find their way around.)

Again I quote Sion:

"No good maps exist of the tangled motorbike tracks and sporadic hamlets from which labouring mothers travel when deliveries go wrong.

Today we started an innovative new project with Mission Morogoro, Hands 4 Africa, Ammalife and Google Maps to accurately map these distant settlements. We are visiting settlements by motorbike, recording coordinates and hearing the stories of the most important people – the remarkable mothers who brave childbirth in a mud house, by kerosene lamplight, hours from medical help.

"The battle against maternal mortality starts with finding, listening and working with these women. Only then can we bring these communities into the fold of the hospital, working with them as equal partners. But ultimately it starts with the map."

Sion highlights in his messages the awful consequences of the bridge collapse and the repercussions on the hospital. It is a double whammy: the patients cannot get there, so income cannot be generated to pay staff; meanwhile, the bill for bringing in drugs and other resources has gone through the roof, because of the hundreds of kilometres detour on bad roads the transport from Morogoro has to take.

My own hospital in Coventry is six times the size of Berega, and its annual budget is £1billion. Berega's budget is less than £150,000. (£1,000 per year is a good salary in rural Tanzania). To save you doing the maths, that means that we in the UK are spending 1,000 times more per bed on the hospital – not counting GPs and all the other available health facilities. Nevertheless, in Tanzania this money is increasingly impossible to find with the bridge down. And no money means no malaria drugs, no antibiotics, no staff – lives will be lost.

The bridge, however, will be rebuilt this year, and we must be ready to continue our impetus in helping make childbirth and childrearing the beautiful and safe experience we should like it to be.

We have begun the process of empowering women, and there is nothing in this continent more likely to produce good. I really hope that Mary, Queen of Scots, will be smiling down on our efforts.

Agnostic Oats

What's in a name?

When they were setting up Amazon, there was a competition to decide the name. They wanted something that would convey the ideas of selling, quality, value and quick delivery. My suggestion was 'We-sell-quality-stuff-cheaply-and-get-it-to-you-quick' but, in an uncharacteristic moment of corporate short-sightedness, they decided not to go with it. They chose 'Amazon' instead. They reckoned that the implied ideas of massive and endless flow of life-giving fresh water, carrying with it the capacity to cut travelling times and difficulties, might give the customers the right feel.

Furthermore, of course the Amazons were the only race ever known in which the women had the power. If an Amazon wanted a new warrior outfit, and wanted it quickly, she would simply summon her fastest slave, and dispatch him to Byzantium with a few drachma captured from a Trojan on her last trip to the coast. With a hurried "I hear and obey!", off he would trot, not resting until his mistress was slaughtering the Phrygians dressed in this summer's colours. The name 'Amazon', then, for an on-line selling company, not only gives off an aroma of all the glories of the largest river in the world – fresh, all-compassing, problem-solving – but also has a hint of unfettered freedom for women. Had the largest river in the world been called 'Attila', doubtless my suggested name for the emporium would have had more chance.

The bottom line is that names matter. Gorbachev needed 'glasnost' to tackle the more sinister aspects of the USSR. Lincoln needed 'emancipation' to free the slaves. Ferguson needed 'Manchester United' to persuade plutocrats to part with eight-figure sums. Had Hamilton Academicals had a similar run of success to United, they perhaps would have run into merchandising difficulties. To drive the point home, would the US defence output be quite as awe-provoking if, instead of being generated in the magical Pentagon, it came instead from the Dodecahedron?

And so it was that the name 'Embrace' evolved to convey a bold attempt to reduce the wastage of life in rural Tanzania. It stands for 'Empowering Women and Children to Receive Adequate Care and Equality', and it endeavours to do what it says on the tin. The idea of caring and collaboration that the word conveys adds exactly the right flavour.

However, of course it only does so in English. In Morogoro region, English is the third language, and Swahili is the common tongue. The nearest word to 'embrace' in Swahili is '*embamba*', which means 'thin'. Not ideal.

On 9 April, the whole management team of Berega hospital met, with one purpose: to come up with a Swahili name for Embrace. The fact that they did so, by the way, is a tribute to their growing excitement that this might truly be the start of something important for the families of the area, for women and for childbirth. That excitement is due in no small part to the widespread support in this country for the idea of Embrace. The meeting was a success, and Embrace is now 'Embrace - *Tushikamane*: 'We are in solidarity'. I append Sion's email below.

So what's in a name? The answer is that a name helps people to share the same view, to build up impetus and, where there is something to be done, to take a fresh look.

Sion's email of April 9 2014: The birth of '*Tushikamane*':

> "After much animated discussion in the management meeting today we have decided on an overall Swahili project name for Embrace: '*Tushikamane*'. This means: 'We are together – in solidarity'

> "The subtitle is: '*Kupunguza vifo vya wajawazito na watoto*' which means: reducing deaths in pregnancy and childhood.

> "We liked that it expressed the sentiment that we want to work in solidarity with the mothers, the village leaders, the fathers and the TBAs in improving the safety of delivery and early years care. Even the HIV programme '*tunajali*' (we care) is a bit paternalistic, so the tone we are setting is one of cooperation. It was agreed by all Swahili speakers that the term would sit well in the minds of the people we wish to work with, and would send out a strong diplomatic message.

> "Dr Abdallah came up with the title, chosen after contributions from all management members, and we all worked on the subtitle.

Hope you like it!

Sion

Tushikamane! I hope you are too!

Post script from Sion: Embrace / *Tushikamane* begins

"The Embrace project is all about reducing maternal and child deaths in rural Tanzania by empowering local experienced midwives and nurses to work with local women and village leaders. Through listening to the problems faced by local women, and in turn working with them on education, capacity building and removal of barriers to access care, we are sure that together we can bring the maternal mortality rates down.

Today was an important first stage - we met three village leaders from Tunguli: Abdallah Mngoya, Ehudi Sangali, Michael Bomphe. Tunguli is an isolated settlement, far from the hospital, accessible only by crossing rivers in a four-wheel drive, or on foot.

We arrived, wary, diplomatic, gauging to what extent the leaders were willing to start a working relationship with us. We needn't have been cautious. On arrival, they presented us with a list of ideas about how we might be most effective and the best ways to engage the different ethnic groups in the area.

We discussed the project name - *Tushikamane* in Kiswahili. This means "We are in solidarity".

Their smiles broadened. "When can you start?'"

Teacher's Recipe

Take 1 kg of strong bread flour with 625 ml of warm water; add a little sugar and touch of salt. Mix them well, forcing the ingredients to intermingle fully. Bake until golden brown, glazing with honey when nearly ready.

You have just made yourself a lovely golden brown brick. Perfect for building biodegradable dwellings, but not so good to eat. If you wanted bread, you missed out the yeast. There is just a little of it, but without *Saccharomyces cerevisiae* – and some careful and sensitive handling – the dough never quite manages to make the miraculous journey to loaf. There has got to be a metaphor in there somewhere.

On a related theme, this is a recipe from 1962: take 10 million people in a massive country with 20 main rivers; add a little foreign investment and a touch of natural resources. Blend in Julius ('Teacher') Nyerere. Intermingle with firm, careful and sensitive handling, glazing with a new constitution when nearly ready. What you get is a mixed legacy, but for all the difficulties and disagreements, it is at least a country still at peace two generations later. More impressively, it is a country where the tribes and religions often work side by side.

Corruption is there, but not on bad African scale. Death is often at the door, and poverty is desperate, but that owes much to the lack of investment and infrastructure (and to Africa's most dangerous animal – the mosquito. Mankind is only number two.) Muslims aspire to send their girls to school just as much as Christians do – though in rural areas, lack of just about everything too often precludes it.

By contrast, in neighbouring Zimbabwe, Nyerere's contemporary is presiding over a country with 8,000% inflation. Prostitution has become a common means of paying for what the developed world takes for granted – education, opportunity, even food. Opponents are crushed ruthlessly and inter-tribal violence is a way of life. For a week-long wedding for his daughter, former Zimbabwean president Robert Mugabe paid out what would have been a year's wages for more than 1,000 of his countrymen.

Leadership. Two very similar countries: two very different directions. Is it too much to say that leadership is at the heart of all collective success –

and atrocity? (My family might disagree in relation to the latter, with the memory of some of my culinary atrocities still emblazoned on their taste-buds. I would point out to them, however, that leadership was not the problem. There was no heady rhetoric. There was no call-to-arms. No-one marched on the presidential palace. Just me, the internet and the misreading of the recipe. Several times. Even my family must admit that some good things came out of it though, such as the widespread acceptance now that curry paste has no place in sweet-and-sour salmon *en croute* with mushy peas.)

Success, then, depends not just on the right recipe, but on the person who catalyses the entire process. Berega hospital has a wonderful leader - Rev Isaac Mgego MBA. Like Nyerere, he came up from the grassroots of the country. He was the first in his family ever to complete high school and the only one in his district ever to make university. Indeed he is one of the few from his village who was even literate. He had to wait for his education until the responsibilities of being a healthy son afforded him the time to go and burn charcoal to pay his way.

Now the Anglican minister and the Muslim medic together try to lead the hospital's response to the health needs of a quarter to half a million people, spread over a vast area, with almost no resources. In a continent of much uncertainty, one thing is sure: without them, Berega would fizzle into the same sleeping sickness which afflicts health services in many rural areas.

So my question is this: out in the community, who will be the one to muster the fight against maternal and child death? Where is the leadership going to come from to tackle the multiple and complex deprivations suffered in Africa's villages? We know that the way ahead lies with empowerment of women, starting with nurturing the development of women's groups. But without leadership, nothing will happen. Who will be rural Tanzania's champion?

The answer came to me as I wrote the question: to lead the fight against the problems of rural African women, we need a rural African woman. Someone who has had to carry precious, dirty water many miles. Someone who has gone hungry to feed a family. Someone who knows what it feels like to watch the motorbike come back with the mother strapped on and the baby poignantly absent.

Money and resources have been what traditionally held us back. However, with the widespread involvement of many good people in

Embrace / *Tushikamane*, perhaps in future the dough will not be the issue. Teacher Nyerere knew the recipe. Let's start looking for the yeast.

Bah! Bar black sheep?

In May, in Berega's territory, four more mothers and dozens of children will have died needlessly of preventable causes while, from 5,000 miles away, we try to help to make a difference. If we give up, the weary fall-back position is that neither culture will mind much and, historically at least, neither will do much. Why have cultures had such a tendency to let things be? Why is inertia such a powerful force, when it doesn't even exist?

Why do some cultures tolerate inappropriate death, inefficiency and corruption?

In the UK, we have an expression 'the black sheep of the family'. It refers to people whose waywardness or disreputability makes their elderly aunts rarely talk to them. Black sheep are barred from the cosiness of social acceptability. Is it not strange, though, that black sheep are not prized? They are unusual and striking animals – precious offspring arising from a rare genetic event. And yet shepherds, far from valuing these future stain-proof garments, traditionally regard them as a bad omen.

The reality is that we humans have a tendency – like sheep – to do what those around us are doing; and if that means being woolly, saying "Baa" and looking for grass in a blizzard on a hillside, then that's what most of us will do. We learn to tolerate what should really be intolerable, and to be blind to what is plainly visible. Even when it might be for our own good to challenge the status quo, an invisible force shuts our mouths and stills our passions. We have, it seems, a deep-felt and powerful need to conform to societal norms, irrespective of the advantages of sometimes breaking the mould. (Breaking the mould, by the way, can indeed be good and yet unappreciated. Einstein, for instance, was an off-the-wall genius who profoundly influenced the sum of human knowledge. And yet, in an irony of relativity, he was shunned by his elderly aunts.)

On the other hand, it is true, of course, that, in many cases, this communal disdain for those who do it differently is well-founded. Society often stands for what is right and wholesome, and waywardness can mean social irresponsibility – a failure to put the community's needs before one's own. In such situations, being wayward will seem to most group members not just inappropriate, but actually immoral. In this way, different versions of morality grow up, fed by a bespoke mixture of tolerance, intolerance and inertia.

My point, however, is that society sometimes gets it wrong. It tolerates what should not be tolerated, and those who stand out from the herd are wrongly regarded as black sheep, even though their take may be the right one. In the Cities of the Plain in the days of Lot and Abraham, those who welcomed visitors with fruit scones, a nice cup of tea and Gomorrah merchandising, were in the small minority. And yet history now unequivocally plumps for their approach as being more conducive to a healthy tourist industry. Sometimes unhelpful or unsavoury codes of behaviour creep into a culture and, without even realising that not everybody invades-others-countries-in-order-to-manipulate-world-power, suddenly it is a matter of popular pride to do so. We knuckle under, and find ourselves doing what, in another epoch or other corner of the world, might be considered ill-mannered at best, or positively immoral at worst. The way-it-is determines the way-it-should-be.

(In middle-class English households like mine, for instance, it is a brave and aberrant husband who stands up against the tyranny of having to make conversation instead of doing important stuff.)

The end result of this natural phenomenon is that polar opposite cultures can emerge, where what is anathema in one society is perfectly acceptable in another, and vice versa. When Victorian missionaries' wives first went to Africa, some were more affronted by the bare breasts than by the paganism. In a similar vein, in our culture now, eating meat is perfectly acceptable. But to many well-informed and well-motivated eco-warriors, it is worse than unethical. I eat my sausage sandwich with alacrity, common assent, and brown sauce, but in a hippy/New Age commune, most inmates would see things very differently:

"Hi Meadow-Lark. Have you seen Gaia anywhere?"
"Yes, Buddica. I think she's in the cow-home."
(Buddica goes to cow home and finds Gaia.)
"Gaia! What in Ashtanga's name are you doing?"
"Oh, hi mum. I'm just cutting Bessie's throat. I fancied sneaking some first-class protein into our nut roast. We may be short of yoghurt for a while."

To us in the north-west quadrisphere, the same outrage is provoked by the inefficiency, inertia and corruption we find in the cultures of far too many low-income countries. This week, I learned that the Tanzanian government agency responsible for paying for certain of Berega's staff and services, has once again failed to come up with the cash. At the same time, the national power grid engineers visited to link up all the staff houses to the grid, but seemed to get equal job satisfaction from not connecting all the staff houses to the grid.

We cannot be too hasty, however, in judging the unacceptable face of an alien culture, for fear that the alien culture might point out our own more dubious excesses. What's more, maybe if we only earned $2 a day, out of which we had to bribe people to pay for basic needs, we might not feel so self-assured about the immorality of trousering the odd back-hander.

I cannot help feeling, however, an overwhelming and determined passion that Tanzania – and indeed the world – might be rid of such nonsense. This mouldy infestation of our planet needs many more mould-breakers: more Einsteins, more non-talkative husbands, and more of the nicer sort of black sheep.

One Direction

Where is your life going?

Three years ago, the answer to this for Niall, Zayn, Liam, Harry and Louis seemed to be: "Nowhere". The singers were headed out of the glamour of the X-Factor talent show, and back into the anonymous twilight of open-mike nights and high-rise hair competitions.

But then they were thrown a life-line: they could re-enter the X-Factor, but only if they joined together to become a boyband, and only if they called it 'One Direction'. They did; and they did. And they did very well. In fact, if you are a pre-pubescent girl, the chances are that you sip your cocoa from a One Direction mug; that you seek comfort in their music when your dad is being so unfair; and that your sleepover is under the watchful vigilance of five guardian-angels smiling down from the wall.

Fairy-tale success. But then Stephen Covey could have taught Simon Cowell a thing or two about 'One Direction'. The 'One Direction' concept is one of the Seven Habits of Highly Effective People. Stephen Covey's seminal book has sold 15 million copies in more tongues than there are mouths, and it articulates the secrets of success of human endeavour.

His first of the seven habits is to suggest that the readers get off their butts and get moving. Immediately thereafter, Stephen adds the second habit: that they should know where they are going. One Direction. The rest, by comparison, is easy.

(By the way, even if Stephen Covey thought of the idea of 'One Direction' first, and so maybe had a right to that poster wall-space, I have to agree with Simon that Niall and the lads have greater merchandising potential. Stephen may be a super-legend but, to a teenage girl weeping into her cocoa, he looks like everyone's dad.)

Anyway, the point is this: five directions, five relative failures. One Direction; one massive success.

The reason for stepping out onto this philosophical path is that last week I had to explain Embrace-*Tushikamane* to a willing but perspicacious male-only audience:

- that we were intending to tackle the awful death rates of mothers and children in rural Tanzania;
- that the roots were deep and complex;
- that shipping in foreign aid to prop up the situation only seemed to produce a temporary benefit; and
- that the evidence was emerging that setting up women's groups, and allowing them to set the agenda seemed to produce a lasting benefit, and an ever up-surging thirst for progress.

At first, I had no problem with this. Empowerment of women in the world would redirect our attention from war and waste to the things that matter. That will save lives.

But then a thought hit me: men also want water. And sanitation. And a clinic. And transport. And healthy children. Am I saying that when men express the need for a well or a toilet or an ambulance, things go wrong? It needs women to spell it out before it will work?

Nevertheless, it is so clear that empowerment of women through women's groups is the way ahead, that the World Health Organisation has now issued official guidance on the importance of this methodology in reducing death in rural Africa:

http://apps.who.int/iris/bitstream/10665/127939/1/9789241507271_eng.pdf?ua=1

So we have a puzzle: why are women's voices more magical, more effective? What is it about enlivening the animation of an uneducated rural African mum, that lights the fuse of an explosion of development?

I had to think long and hard. I have known many rural African women but, as an urban European male, I think differently. What is wrong with my way of thinking? What is wrong with men? (My wife, looking over my shoulder, says "How much time have you got?")

And then it hit me. In sub-Saharan African villages, men often represent authority and institution. Tradition. The way things are. And in these breathless days of the 21st century, institutions are, in many cases, crumbling, precisely because of being what they are – instead of what they might be.

Institutions are in danger of not getting those first two of Stephen Covey's most important prompts: get moving and know where you are going. Together, on the same journey.

Women talk. They listen to other women talking. (My wife, looking over my shoulder, says "It's not hard.") Rural Tanzanian women fetch the water. They find something to cook. They work. They raise their children and look after them when they are sick. Too often, the women die young. They want a better world, and they are willing to work hard for years, to reach that goal.

Given just a hint of a chance, they will have One Direction.

When they start the journey, we will be there to help.

Whatever ...

When I was a practising obstetrician, helping women to prepare for childbirth was an important part of the job. This especially applies to the birth of the first child, which natural selection, in a harsh and impassive demonstration of its single-mindedness, has made by far the toughest.

Being a left-leaning, feminist, empathic sort of person, with only mild Asperger's syndrome, I might easily have been tempted to recommend that women in labour listen to whale music in a giant tub of yoghurt under an oak tree, with their partners messily massaging the small of their back until second stage kicks in, had it not been for our first child.

Jenny took five days to decide to come out above, rather than below, the bladder. The emergency C-section under general anaesthetic has been a familiar shipwreck of the dreams of far too many couples.

At first, I used to believe that this meant the need for more intense childbirth preparations, particularly in relation to managing one's expectations. Then a weird thing happened. I noticed that those least likely to make such preparations – teenagers from less privileged backgrounds – often had remarkably good labours. When asked in advance what their birth plan was, such a person might typically say, "Whatever …"

Eventually, I stumbled on the obvious answer: it is all about dealing with stress and anxiety. More stress: more adrenaline. More adrenaline: more pain; tighter pelvis; weaker contractions.

More chilled: more natural oxytocin; more compliant pelvis; stronger contractions. More 'whatever'. Childbirth preparation helps, but it does so especially in proportion to the amount it helps you take control, at the same time as relaxing and let it happen. (Easy for a man to say. For a man to write, actually. Asperger's kicking in.)

So I ended up spending a lot of time explaining to first-time mums the need to chill out at home as long as possible, (as long as all was well and the baby was moving normally). Have a bath. Have something to eat. Go for a walk. Watch an East Enders box set. OK, perhaps not East Enders. Anyway, chill. Have the transport ready, then only get in it when you reach the "Get this feckin baby out!" stage.

It shows what an English city-dweller I am, that in all these considerations, it never struck me to doubt that the transport would always be there. Not just the car, but someone to drive it, fuel to put in it, money to pay for it and a short road to drive it along.

This set of thoughts has been flashing through my head because of a recent email from Berega: a bus and car crash near the hospital has led to 49 admissions, many of them critical, in a hospital whose resources are already badly overstretched.

In Tanzania, there are no tarred roads in rural areas. Just dirt roads which get flooded and scarred by the ironic flashes of angry waters through this parched landscape. In 2010, there were 1.24 million deaths on the world's roads, most of them occurring in countries like Tanzania where overcrowded transport, packed with the poor, the needy and the pregnant, recklessly charges towards its destination – or sometimes its destiny.

In the territory of Berega hospital, the problem is made worse by the unaffordability of cars. Bikes and motor bikes are the only ways to make a longer journey, and they are by no means always satisfactory.

My mind goes back to those two most disturbing memories of my time at Berega – both of them relating to transport, rather than health. One was of the woman who came from a distant village on a motorbike having been in labour for five days. For the last three days, the baby's head had been out, and the body still in. In that state, she managed the unimaginable middle passenger journey to reach help. More unimaginable still was the woman who arrived too late, having bled just too much on the bumpy ride in. Her body was taken back to her village and her family, a lifeless middle passenger on a bumpy ride back.

When I went to Tanzania, I had imagined that health services were the central plank in the strategy for saving mothers' lives. But just as the causes of death are complex, so are the solutions. Fabulous maternity services that no-one can reach, that no-one can afford, will save no-one's lives. Whatever we do, it has to involve community development. It has to address, more urgently perhaps than any health priority, those issues which prevent access to care: for instance poverty, lack of female education and poor transport.

Whatever solutions exist must (the WHO now tells us) be first articulated by the village women themselves if they are to be pursued sustainably:

http://apps.who.int/iris/bitstream/10665/127939/1/9789241507271_eng.pdf?ua=1

Whatever we do, we must get out into communities and engage with pregnant women and their sisters and their carers, if we do not want them to become next year's mortality statistics. Whatever these mums feel might be the solutions, be it to poverty or education or transport, those are the directions in which we must travel.

Whatever.

In the Dog House

For consumers of the annals of human endeavour, two memorable morsels ricocheted around the social media last weekend. The one you are less likely to have sampled is the sight of Queen Elsa pouring an ice-bucket over the head of a well-meaning but gullible ex-obstetrician:

https://www.youtube.com/watch?v=FBvbg3yeslo

The intention was to raise funds to stop mothers dying in childbirth; to give hope to communities in rural Tanzania; to help a part of the world where each village has ten children die every year:

http://yellowchuckchucks.blogspot.co.uk/2014/09/what-size-for-womens-groups-in-rural.html
http://yellowchuckchucks.blogspot.co.uk/2014/08/embrace-tushikmanane-where-we-are.html

However, nothing much seems to be happening on the fundraising site, and the story more likely to have captured your attention was the burning down of the dogs' home in Manchester. The home is a sort of refuge for dogs, where they can find friendship; comfort; chair-legs smelling of other dogs' urine; and, if needed, counselling. It is a sign of a deeply sophisticated society that we care in this way for a species that has brought to ours so much in the way of comfort, unquestioning friendship and chewed sticks. I have noticed in my short transit through life on earth, that a person who is kind to humans is rarely cruel to animals.

Looking after dogs, then, is a noble enough undertaking, and it would not have been surprising to have observed generous support after the home was tragically struck by such a devastating fire. What was more than surprising – even astonishing, indeed 'Blairs-decide-to-retire-to-holiday-home-in-Merthyr-Tydfil' level of unlikeliness – was that, in just a single weekend, they raised £1.2 million for the re-building of the dogs' home.

I know that my ice-bucket challenge did not tap into the same market. I do not have the same appeal as a puppy: apart from the lower half of my face, I am not furry; I do not have wistful eyes; and I bite when tickled.

There's more:

- If someone throws a tennis ball, I am perfectly capable of almost completely ignoring it.
- I am not intrigued by the smell of other people's trousers.
- If I find anything disgusting while walking through the park, I am neither tempted to eat it nor to roll in it.
- I am allowed on the sofa.

I could go on, but I am conceding the point that I lack the canine X factor. In a head-to-head fund-raiser between Lassie and me, to buy somewhere to rest our weary heads, the collie-dog would have the donors rounded up before I had even downloaded the Lottery's "Fifteen Things You Should Know Before Applying For An Ageing Hippy Weary Cranium Residence-Enhancement Grant".

But what would Lassie think about spending that amount on her home, at the cost of her owner's life, and those of her children? If dogs really are a person's best friend, would they truly want to move into million-pound kennels when, 5,000 miles away, the young lads who would love to scamper with them are beset by malaria, malnutrition, infestations, infections and tragedy – and who, much too often, will never throw a stick again.

I do not exempt myself from this sobering reflection. What I have spent on our two dogs this last dozen years would have paid for many wells. For a school perhaps. For a Land Rover ambulance. For many, many emergency C-sections, performed in poor light on mothers desperate to survive and see their child.

Where would we be, though, if suddenly we were equitable in the distribution of our largesse? That simply would not work without unravelling the society we live in. Theme parks and cinemas would close down as pleasure-seekers found new comfort in sending their spare cash to the needy. The clothing industry would grind to a halt as we wore what we wore until it fell off our backs, giving the money released to the naked and the cold. Malbec producers would call an emergency summit in Mendoza, as I replaced my nightly nectar with enough dirty water to moisten my mouth.

The world is not fair and never will be. For there to be wealth-sharing, there has to be wealth.

But, on the other hand, where would we be, in this tragically unequal world, if we closed our ears to the anguish of death and tragedy, albeit in distant lands? Where would we be if the cries of the suffering and the desperate never penetrated our cocoon? Where would Lassie be if, knowing that all this was going on in the world, she accepted a millionaire's kennel?

For me, dog-lover though I am, I know where I would be if I ignored humanity in favour of other species.

In the dog house.

To be a girl

'To be a girl' is a wonderful campaign launched by Water Aid:

https://www.youtube.com/watch?v=ljhs6YEVCAw#t=24

It highlights the mediaeval task-list that gets handed out to children across the world, along with their two X chromosomes. For girls, from as soon as they are no longer carried, they carry.

They carry water, babies or often both, and they do so from an early age. Weighing down your head with water many times a day becomes a substitute for school, where you otherwise might have weighed down your head with something altogether more useful and liberating. And school is where you might have hoped to be a girl – a child being cared for, instead of one doing the caring.

(As a non-girl, I have here to say that we males also suffer our unfairnesses. One of these is that girls routinely outperform us when they do get to school:

http://www.dailymail.co.uk/sciencetech/article-2616906/Boys-perform-worse-girls-EVERY-school-subject-100-years-claims-study.html

In the article quoted, they put this down to learning styles, and I think that there might be something in that. My daughters' learning style was to listen to the teacher and participate in class, then after school to do their homework. It seemed to work for them, I must admit.)

Nevertheless, the sad fact is that millions of girls, even in the 21st century, never experience the luxury of having a teacher to listen to. The insidiously grave consequences for the world of this huge burden of unfairness go way beyond the problem of sexism. It is true, of course, that girls and women are far more likely to be oppressed – or suppressed – by the opposite gender, but the origin of enforced girl-labour is not archetypally sexist in the way we now define it. It is cultural, and that makes it much more difficult to undo: The division of labour between males and females in under-developed rural settings was a practical response to the challenges of Africa. In general, in centuries gone by, men were more suited to hunting and to protecting livestock and families. Women were more suited to child-rearing. This culture was just accepted and put up with courageously. Then, as now, for many put-upon women, laughter and song were never far from the lips, just as tragedy and hardship were never far from the door. The realities of life.

However, in this more enlightened age, we have the opportunity – indeed a duty – to deal with the realities of death. In rural Tanzania, a peaceful country, approximately one in 30 women can expect to die prematurely related to conception and childbirth. 99% of these deaths would not have happened, had the birth occurred in the UK. One in 10 children dies before the age of five. The causes of child death are also poignantly preventable: birth complications, malnutrition, malaria, pneumonia, diarrhoea and infectious diseases (TB, HIV, measles, meningitis, whooping cough, tetanus).

For Europeans, it might seem that this is a comfortably distant problem needing a little humanitarian handout. For others, this particular pebble makes no ripple on their pond. That is a precariously blinkered view, however. Bear in mind, that no cosseted comfort of a rich civilisation ever lasted more than a few centuries. Every so often in the history of mankind, there is an 'adjustment' with a regression to the mean. For much of humanity, we are currently living through such an adjustment, whereby our European level of privilege is dropping towards the world average. How awfully far we have to fall, if we do not do something to bring up the underprivileged underclass, who even now, far too often, sell all they have to pay bad people to despatch them from the African to the European coast.

What can be done? Well, reading the list of causes of death, you would be forgiven for thinking that the solutions were uncomplicated, relatively cheap and surely manageable, even in rural Africa. Family planning for a start. In a setting where six babies is the average, reducing this to two or three would deal a hefty blow to both maternal and child mortality, at the same time as reducing HIV. Immunisation would pick up half the list, and better nutrition, more breast-feeding and better management of pregnancy and childbirth would complete the decimation of disasters.

Well you would be right. In fact, the World Health Organisation agrees with you. What's more, the whole planet agrees with you, and said so nearly four decades ago in the Declaration of Alma Ata:

http://www.who.int/social_determinants/tools/multimedia/alma_ata/en/

What happened? I'll tell you what happened. This did:

Plus ça change…

Instead of going to school, she did jobs. If she grows up, she will not know anything about Alma Ata. Immunisation and antenatal care and condoms and antibiotics and micro-nutrition will be part of a tapestry of irrational aversions in her culturally-attuned mind.

Despite many heartening successes and steadily improving averages, simple health care messages cannot be 'done' to a village or its people. Sustainable progress is based on understanding and self-determination, and that in turn depends on female education. Without the mothers themselves understanding what is needed, and without women chivvying for it, nothing much progresses in the villages of rural Africa.

That is why Embrace-*Tushikamane* seeks first to empower women to understand and prioritise their problems, before helping them to respond.

So … to be a girl. If you want to know what it means to be a girl in Mnafu, you'll have to ask one. Within this generation, you might be able to do so in a much more meaningful way and get a response, for the first time in history, full of hope for the community.

Normal Distribution

Half the women attending antenatal care in rural Tanzania are less than average weight. Interestingly, however, this percentage is exactly the same in UK antenatal clinics. Does this mean that poor nutrition is no more an issue in African villages than it is in the UK?

(OK, just to explain, for those reading this book over an emergency cup of coffee and a bleary breakfast, half of any mathematical group is below average, and the other half above, with no floating voters.)

Facts never lie. But neither do they always stand up to close scrutiny. It should not surprise you, of course, that 50% of women will be 'underweight', if by this you mean that they are under the average. By definition, half of Tanzanian women will be below the Tanzanian average, and half above. The same logic applies to the UK. The true fact is, of course, that, by UK standards, far too many rural Tanzanian women are malnourished.

My point is that I could. if I chose, weave the words to support whichever tapestry of beliefs I subscribed to. Vital as facts might be, they are worse than useless without correct interpretation, and most of us have a touch of dyscalculia when it comes to interpreting scientific advance. The packaging of the stats-message often matters considerably more than what you find if you can be bothered to take off the wrappings. Present the message well, and the whole world is listening.

Because of this, for instance, people now spend more than £20 billion a year on statins. In more than 95% of cases, these statins do no good whatever and, in some cases, they do harm. (Notice my clever packaging of the anti-statin message, and please don't stop taking them if you need them. I was just making a point. You do not know which group you are in. Harm is rare, and life-saving frequent.)

But it is indeed a hugely important point: at this rate of headstrong and introspective spending, in the 30 years it takes generation X to pass to the next axis, the world will have spent £600 billion on statins – almost all of it 'wasted'. That would pay for everyone on the planet, every single soul, to have, for instance, safe water and sanitation; or an iPad-mini; or a luxury overnight trip for two on the Manchester Ship Canal from Thelwall Viaduct to Weaver Sluice.

How in heaven's name do we prioritise our collective spending like this? The answer is that we are too ready to believe what we are told. When an expensive drug or gadget comes along, we can be tantalised and seduced into believing that we cannot live without it. Or, when a cheap or even cost-neutral bit of sense tries to influence the way we live, we can be too eager to dismiss it as 'unproven'. (It took 30 years, for instance, from the first evidence that smoking was bad for you, for the message to be routinely adopted by doctors. It took even more than 30 years in the case of the deleterious effects of too much sugar. And, on a personal note, it has taken even more years again for me to assimilate the data that Malbec may not completely wipe out the harm done to one's metabolism by sausages. And I'm still not 100% convinced …)

So here's the rub: we need information, and we need it to be well-interpreted, in order to legitimise and optimise our use of resources.

We need it, but we don't often get it, and so our choices can be skewed.

This need for the naked truth is particularly the case when our enthusiasm to do the right thing blinds us to potential negative effects of our actions. Our experience of anecdotal benefit and our anticipation of success might too easily get in the way of learning proper lessons about what we have been doing. In the last generation or two of aid from the privileged to the under-privileged nations, these lessons have often had to be learnt more than once. As a result, for instance, every armchair philanthropist now knows that we have to teach people to fish, rather than giving them their daily mackerel, (a philosophy yet to bear much fruit in some parts of the Sahara). The dissipation of overseas aid and goodwill by ineptitude is still too common a phenomenon in Africa. The rocks of inefficiency and corruption can shipwreck good-hearted dreams, and the swirling currents of perverse incentives and political expediency can cause many a good scheme to founder.

I am building up to identifying a critical insight about the Embrace-*Tushikamane* project: We need to be careful that we are using the resources to best effect.

Part of the answer is evaluation of impact: did we save lives? Without doing much harm? However, even such a seemingly simple parameter of measurement is a sophisticated business, needing careful thought. If, for instance, as a response to the problems identified by women's groups, we implement an improved transport system, linked to training of traditional birth attendants to know which women to send in, then many more women might arrive at the hospital gates, including those who previously would have died at home on the bloody floor of their hut, or under the grubby lantern of a despairing attendant. The project might therefore, at first, seem to be delivering more death in hospital – but less in the community. Indeed, there may be far less overall, without this being apparent. These are tough issues needing a professional response.

Meanwhile, let me finish by arguing with myself a little. Let's face it, I am the only one authorised to write in my own book, and there is therefore the danger of portraying just one view of the topic. Fortunately, in this case I disagree wholeheartedly with myself, if I am trying to say that scientific evaluation is only about stats and normal distributions.

Statistics are vital, but so is narrative and observation of what happens. Stats could tell you that your results fall way outside the normal distribution, and that something unusual is happening. But they will not tell you why, so you might not be able to replicate success nor to rectify what seems like failure. An analogy: your data tells you that none of your flat-packed IKEA furniture seems to stay up long after you reconstruct it. Number-crunching reveals that not a single item in your new bedroom suite withstood the weight of (respectively) an ironically full cup of coffee, an inquisitive cat, and a weary, end-of-day backside. What these stats do not explain to you is that hammers do not work on screws. Observation of what is happening can be as important as measuring the degree to which it happened.

And here is a further complexity: there will be times in science when numbers will be not just inadequate, but utterly beyond inadequate to tell the story. When Copernicus inferred that the earth revolved around the sun, he did not need to check a representative number of solar systems to ensure that his conclusion reached statistical significance. When Watson and Crick tracked down the structure of DNA, they did not have to repeat the task with other molecules to prove it was not a fluke. At the heart of science is observation, combined with understanding about what you are seeing. Statistics are just a means to that end.

Numbers are important. Vital. But we should use the right tool for the right purpose. Sometimes it is analysis of data, followed by wise inference. Sometimes it is insightful observation and description. Sometimes, even science is inadequate to encapsulate wisdom, and only poignancy can capture the moment. I remember many, many times, too many to count, when I have had the privilege of saving a woman's life and delivering a baby into her desperate and exhausted arms, and neither numbers nor words would suffice in describing what just happened.

So let me finish with an example of charitable intervention in Africa which reconciles all of these quandaries, which observes, measures, understands, adjusts – and delivers where it matters. In the last chapter, I mentioned Water Aid's wonderful To Be A Girl campaign, to provide villages with water so that the girls can be freed to live more appropriate lives. The campaign recently wrapped up, and if you don't cry when you watch the video, you get your money back:

https://www.youtube.com/watch?v=Op4Lopax3EAandlist=UU3JVuo2A_Am7XW5tkFZRi5A

In African development, things can grind to ignominious and poorly understood defeat, under a wrapping of dyscalculia, or they can work wonderfully. Water Aid is one of the successes, and water distribution is the foundation of future possibility – along with education, food, transport, community health, and eradication of extreme poverty. These are the most basic of human needs, sadly lacking throughout much of Africa. Embrace-Tushikamane seeks, in one small part of the planet anyway, to turn under-development into normal distribution.

Missing the point

This would be a typical conversation with one of my daughters, when she was coming in late as a teenager:

Me: "Do you know what the time is?"
Her: "….(wordless scorn plus weary sigh plus angry face) ….
Me: "Well, I'll tell you. It's nearly one o'clock in the morning."
Her: "….(scoffing sigh plus angry face, plus sharp downblast of air via the nostrils) ….
Me: (in conciliatory tone) "We've been really worried…"
Her: "….(disbelieving guttural sound plus angry face, plus sharp downblast of air via the nostrils, plus anguished groan) ….
Me: "And you promised you'd be in by midnight …"
Her: "….(incredulous snort plus angry face, plus sharp downblast of air via the nostrils, plus muttering about not believing this) …. "
Me: (pleading) "We've been through all this …"
Her: (with withering, piercing, impatience at my imbecility) "What's your point???"

It seemed that I was missing the point. It was unjust of me, I was made to understand, to expect that she should leave her friends just when they all were having a good time. Why didn't I just trust her?

Now, a decade or more later, it's all worked out very well indeed and, what's more, this nocturnal training has left me well-briefed in the need to get to the point quickly. (A lesson made the harder to implement because of my irresistible tendency to make room for important asides.)

So what's my point in bringing this up? It is this: that justice appears not to be an absolute, but seems instead to depend on where you are standing.

Take the land of the Maasai, for instance – which is what the Tanzanian government is trying to do, in part at least. The Loliondo territory is within 'Maasailand' and has been coveted by the Ortelo Business Corporation, a safari company set up by a UAE official close to the Dubai royal family. They want to turn it into an exclusive opportunity to kill the things that make the place particularly special:

The Maasai are objecting, and they have a point: They are one of the original tribes of East Africa, and they have been in this land for the last two or three centuries. It happens, however, that their homeland borders on one of the world's greatest game reserves – the Serengeti. Loliondo is 1,500 sq km smack in the middle of the Maasai traditional lands – and right next-door to the national park. But from the government's point of view, is this indeed Maasai-owned territory? The obvious interpretation would be that of course it is theirs, based on the (admittedly colonially-unsound) reason that they have lived there for so long. It is where their homes are. Their villages. Their scrub-land. Their water-holes. Their holy places. It is where the bones of their ancestors bleach in the sun. It is where their tumble-down mud dwellings are, from which the men head out into the wild bush in order to graze their cattle.

Another point of view, however, and another version of the justice of the situation, is that the land is not theirs at all. It belongs to the family of Tanzania. The government owns all the land. (But let's not stray too far into politics, here. OK, just a bit, then. In 1967, six years after coming to power, socialist president Julius Nyerere signed the Arusha Declaration, whereby '*Ujamaa*' or 'Being a family', became the dominant Tanzanian policy. Collective farms forcibly replaced previous settlements, and many resources, including land, were nationalised, leading to widespread corruption and sometimes desperate privation.

At the same time, however, health and education took a major leap forwards. Nyerere was a devout, honest and good-hearted man, and his dedication – to freedom, unity, and family – lives on in many a hip-hop rap, a legacy he encouraged. Ultimately, however, for the large majority of the population, poverty and dependency were the outcome, as well as, technically, lack of individual ownership of their traditional lands.) So the government sees itself as having every right to use the land in whatever way it chooses, because the Maasai do not own it. Their point is that tourism would be good for the nation. And it has, of course, offered to compensate the Maasai with money (£10 a head).

However, money does not buy existence, and existence is what the Maasai would not have in any other setting. Where could they go with the cattle? Where could they go without cattle? It is like clearing 40,000 of us out of a leafy suburb in Surrey, leaving behind our homes and livelihoods, and re-settling us in a trailer park in those parts of the Severn Estuary not yet permanently under three feet of water. But of course, we would be compensated with £10 per person, so we would not go short of porridge for at least a fortnight.

The point that the government seem to be missing is this: at just around the same time that the displaced Maasai became the centre of an almost irremediable sociological disaster, the world outcry would have reached such a pitch that no-one would dare hunt in the territory anyway. Is there no solution that involves leaving the Maasai where they are, and still taking the lucre of the emir? Surely there is?

I deeply hope the Maasai will win, and I hope as well that you will have the satisfaction of having added your name to the many millions who have already signed petitions.

But if they do stay where they are, don't let me leave you with the impression that Maasai life is an endless whirl of fun.

("Let's camp here for the night then, Miterienanka. I'll light a fire, 'cos I noticed a lion behind that bush, eating some missionaries.

"OK, Ntirkana. I'll get the cappuccinos on the go. Cocoa or cinnamon?")

Even when in possession of their land, Maasai have a tough life. So many of their children die soon after birth that they do not even name them until they are three months old. Thereafter, more than one in ten still die before the age of five – malaria, diarrhoea and dehydration, accidents, pneumonia, meningitis, TB etc. In the African bush, with no money, no transport and no privilege, there is nowhere to hide.

Of the girls that survive, they have to marry young, so as to keep the tribe supplied with the next generation. Because they might begin to child-bear too early, far too many of these girls do not even make it past the first delivery. (I saw one close call myself, recorded in an earlier chapter. The frightened 14-year-old was fortunate enough not only to be close to a hospital when she developed her pre-eclampsia, but to be born of parents who understood that nature does not always get it right. When her blood pressure became dangerous to life, I offered her a Caesarean section. The girl's mother refused – "We have to wait until the grandfather sells a cow". In the night, the girl began to fit. If you are going to get full-blown eclampsia in Africa, then do it in hospital, when an obstetrician is visiting. We saved the young mother, and I put the dead baby girl in the arms of the grandmother, who received her gratefully, reverently and with just a bit too much resignation.)

So here's the rub: while government officials are pointlessly planning to betray the country's people and denude the country of its resources, it leaves them little time to deal with the real issues, which are the dreadful and preventable levels of mortality.

Given that the maternal death rate in Loliondo is around 100 times that in London, they are more than missing the point.

New Year's Resolution

I have no excuses for the long gap since the last chapter. I am retired after all, which means that I can resolve to do what I like, as long as it is legal, wise and does not start before 9.30am. Yes, 9.30. For six decades, I have submitted to the tyranny of sunrise, and to its autocratic preoccupation with startling us deep-sleepers from our slumber. What's more, sunrise's little helpers draw perverse pleasure from following up on their mistress's whim. I have been elbowed in the ribs. I have had the covers yanked from the jelly that will later be myself. I have been taunted from across the room by the smug optimism of the radio-alarm. I have begged for just five more minutes to finish a tantalising dream in which I invent an amazing ... (well, of course I can't tell you what it was, because I was woken before the end). In every case, until I retired, sunrise won.

Now, however, in a snoozers' spring that brings hope around the world to those oppressed by Alectrona's despotic grip on the eiderdown, I have broken the yoke.

(Alectrona, by the way, was the Greek goddess of getting up in the morning. Presumably she was in the loo when Zeus was giving out jobs: 'god of the oceans', 'king of the planets', 'god without portfolio' and the like.

"Sorry I'm late, Zeus. Whatcha got?"
"Oh Alectrona! I forgot about you! I was going to give you 'goddess of silent transport', but it's gone. Didn't even hear it go."
"Never mind, Zeus. I'm easy. What's left in the bag?"
"Umm… well actually only … 'goddess of getting up in the morning', 'goddess of toothache', and 'goddess of flat-packed furniture' …"
"You've got to be kidding!" etc)

Anyway, you get the point that, for some of us on the planet, getting up needs to be an altogether more measured process than being unceremoniously decanted into reality, an hour before your metabolism.

Being aware of my surroundings from 9.30am onwards, however, still gives me plenty of time to write the next chapter.

Assuming that I don't hit writer's block …

February 2015: Ah yes. The book. Right, here goes:

A few nights ago I spoke about Embrace-*Tushikamane* to a group of Coventry women belonging to a society called 'The Soroptimists'. It sounded like it should be a society of post-Nostradamus alchemists seeking the Lost Scroll of Soropto so, before I did the talk, I checked out who these people might be. In fact, the word means 'Sisters of excellence' or 'The best for Sisters'. Their website describes their work:

'Soroptimist International is a global volunteer movement working together to transform the lives of women and girls. Our network of around 80,000 club members in 130 countries and territories works at local, national and international level to educate, empower, and enable opportunities for women and girls'.

So I was coming to tell the people who already know, that the solution to the awful inadequacies of rural Africa is empowerment of women and girls. Hmmmm. It seems that there really is nothing new under the sun.

Soroptimists began in 1921 in California, ten years after women got the vote in that state, and one year after women's suffrage was finally won for all women in the USA, after a long and bitter battle. In those days, universal suffrage was felt to be a matter of human rights, but rather impractical. It was going to take some considerable effort and expense to make it happen – like building a house or a school or a road. It transpired, over the next three generations, that this road, far from being impractical, was actually the only road leading from war, intolerance, privation and poverty, to safety, freedom, abundance and justice. Giving a voice to the unempowered, the disenfranchised and the oppressed, turned out to be a rich investment for society.

Such richness is not just societal: a country's actual wealth and life expectancy are directly proportional to the rate of female emancipation. I have mused before in this book, as to why this counter-intuitive ingredient of civilisation's recipe should be so vital. The yang of assertion and seeming-strength has traditionally seemed more worthy of pursuit than the yin of vulnerability and seeming-weakness. But of course, both yin and yang are needed in any sustainable solution. Some Chinese philosophers already understood this balance nearly three millennia ago.

In many rural areas of sub-Saharan African countries, however, the balance of equal gender-opportunity is conspicuous by its absence. In most of these countries, for instance, less than half the girls even finish primary school. Poverty, or domestic duties, or conflict, or betrothal, or even predation separate girls from their potential before even the innocence of their girlhood is over. In the process, the country ironically loses the solutions to the precise problems which tie it to under-development.

Let me give a real example: Jenipher Namutosi. Jenipher lives in a remote village in Uganda where, for three decades, she has fulfilled the traditional role demanded of her. Recently, she had her fifth child and, as often happens with women after their fourth pregnancy, she began to bleed after delivery. This is the commonest cause of maternal death in the world, and one such death happens about every 10 minutes somewhere on the planet. Jenipher was saved by the recent introduction of motor-bike ambulances by a Welsh charity.

Stop and ask yourself, however, how it was that the ambulance, in a country riddled with corruption and inefficiency, was actually available, maintained, fuelled and ready – and how the birth attendant knew when to call for help and what to do, and how the driver was able to deal with what he found. The answer, of course, is that community development in rural Africa simply cannot be unidimensional. You cannot air-drop solutions, then fly off again. Progress has to occur within a matrix of self-determination and community participation – and women's voices are a vital component. Or as the Soroptimists so neatly put it: 'Working together to transform lives…'

It goes without saying that, of course, by including women in the dialogue, a new perspective will take shape. For instance, it will cease to be lost on the community decision-makers that, when you could only have afforded to feed, keep healthy and educate two children, then dying as you give birth to your fifth one might be counter-productive.

Embrace-*Tushikamane* is getting closer – in a painfully slow process – to working alongside a Tanzanian Health and Community Development Institute, to begin establishing women's voices within hamlet and village-based self-determination. Its mission is to set up women's groups in rural Morogoro, beginning in Tunguli.

We in the privileged world need to be there for the villages as they aspire to something better for the future of their communities. As hamlets in rural Tanzania begin to articulate their needs, we need to support organisations such as Mission Morogoro (http://www.missionmorogoro.org.uk/), who are getting ready to support some of the ways in which the community will move into the 21st century.

A shameful loss of mothers and their children continues in rural Africa. We must resolve to help. And help to resolve.

A New Year's resolution?

Every Dog has his Day (and Women have 8 March)

In England, there is a saying: 'Every dog has his day'. It means that, if you are a dog, then sooner or later your time of favour will come. For at least one of your 4,000 days on the planet, you will not be made to sit or do tricks; you will be permitted to eat that deliciously-decaying detritus you found under a bush, and humans will understand the honour you are bestowing when you mark your territory on their trouser leg.

However, I have to say that, for me, the jury is still out on the value of this saying as a piece of proverbial wisdom to pass down the generations:

"Don't worry, son, every dog has his day!"

"Oh thanks Dad! Does that mean that soon I will stop being bullied, and instead will start being appreciated by my teachers, will then have my talents nurtured and eventually will conquer all injustice and settle down to a life of peace and plenty?"

"Er, no son. It means that today, on a special deal which I can offer for one day only, I won't scold you if you chase our cat."

(It is no surprise to me, by the way, that this adage might be of little worth, given that it was popularised by Shakespeare in his play, Hamlet. We are talking about a play in which the hero is named after a cigar or small town; when he's not talking to himself, he talks to ghosts and skulls; he feigns madness by speaking mediaeval English; then everyone dies. This is not the output of a rational mind.)

It is not for its edification, then, that I began thinking about this proverb on International Women's Day last month, but for its subliminal implications. Every dog has its day? All the women on earth get one day on 8 March, but dogs get one each?

But here is an extension of these musings on canine quotas. Being 'a bit of a dog' is something of a backhanded compliment, so I'd be quite content with the comparison, and would get on and have my day. However, if there were a parallel axiom for the female of the species, it would not roll off the tongue quite so well. "Every bitch has her day" doesn't really work as a pick-me-up for the downtrodden. Dog = fine. Bitch = insult. Where does this all come from?

It seems that, right from Saxon times and before, the males of commonly encountered animals had names to be aspired to, macho and manly: stallion, bull, cock, buck, stag, ram, stud, etc. Much of this Teutonic nomenclature legitimately derives from the tendency of male mammals, in due season, when they stop fighting, feasting and farting, to exhibit something of an appetite for cocking, bucking, stagging, studding, ramming and the like. Fair play. We are who we are. Those Saxons called it as they saw it.

By this argument, however, the female Saxon species-names should reflect, by contrast, some feminine qualities. A bull's mate might have been a 'feeder', or 'carer'. A carthorse's companion could perhaps have been a 'toiler'. A fox or dog's life-partner maybe a 'rearer', instead of which, we have 'cow', 'nag', 'vixen' and 'bitch' – to which we could add mare, sow, nanny and hind.

I have a theory as to how this derogatory naming-system came about. Given that Saxon tribes did not speak the same language as Romans, Vikings, Gauls and others around them, it follows that there must have been a time when they were inventing the words for the world they lived in. This presumably happened around the campfire at night-time, when the menfolk got back from procuring, protecting, plundering, and perhaps a touch of *ex tempore* procreating. Perhaps, now and then, they would set an evening aside for naming of one of their livestock.

The women would then of course be tasked with preparing the *cerf en croute,* and would only get a fleeting chance for a chat. Even the hen-pecked warrior would not wish to be late for the nocturnal naming-fest, no matter how much he valued his spouse's view. So you might imagine a conversation like this:

Woman: "O Hunter-man!"
(This is before they had names even for themselves)
Man: "Yes, O Broth-But-Sometimes-Stew-Woman?"
Woman: "Tonight, men at fire are naming our horned-milk-beast!"
Man: "Yes, and me got good idea. Me say call it: 'Bob' …"
Woman: "Hmm… Me no like 'Bob'. Not very female. No. You must call it 'Succa-Succa-Life-Milk'."
Man: "If me call it 'Succa-Succa-Life-Milk', Hunter-Warmen hurt me bad …"

Woman: "If you love me, you call it 'Succa-Succa-Life-Milk' ..."
(Later, after naming fest):
Woman: "O Hunter Man! Why you got only one eye?"
Man: "They're going with 'cow' ..."

As then, now. A barely noticed inequity and imbalance, and yet one which defines and destabilises the very basis of our lives: Men, (well, actually, males, and even then not all of them), when given the authority, the power and a free rein, tend to have a more violent and openly confrontational world view. The result has been a world in which war is more important than water, and cruelty is a stronger currency than caring.

(By the way, if you are a woman reading this, don't get smug. If women alone had the authority, the power and a free rein, the world would still be unbalanced and unstable:

"My Lady! Even now, the enemy are at the gates of the Tower of London!"
"Then haste! Summon my personal guard!"
"The Tofu-Eaters are already in position, Ma'am!"
"Have they their needles?"
"Ready at your command, Ma'am."
"Then let the tapestry begin!"

This is nonsensical stereotyping, of course, but it made me laugh, so I couldn't resist. I just want to say that we share the same differences. What we need, but do not have, is balance.)

But to the serious point: balance. Yin and yang. Competition and cooperation. Determination and concession. The view of those who are running the country and the view of those who are running the home. The perspective of those travelling miles for work and that of those travelling miles for water. The old customs but the new understanding – of society, of family, of health, of disease and of why so many mothers die in childbirth.

Look, it is far, far too much of an over-simplification to suggest that war and violence are man things. But you can't help feeling that many of the most unspeakable excesses that currently plague our news-streams would not be occurring in a world where women had a full say.

What is certainly true is this: in rural Malawian villages where women have found a voice – with the blessing, participation and encouragement of the men – truly wonderful things are happening. The desperate toll of death in childbirth is finally reducing. Please watch again:

http://vimeo.com/12427420

Florida Banda and Mikey Rosato, two of the key players in this transformation, are fully signed up to the Embrace-*Tushikamane* project to spread the development of women's groups into rural Tanzania.

Even as I write, I am waiting for finalisation of the inaugural meeting of Florida with Embrace's Tanzanian partners. The conference will celebrate the success of community participation and women's groups in reducing deaths of mums and babies in the villages of Malawi. Its main focus, however, will be on how to spread the lessons to other countries – especially neighbouring Tanzania, which shares so much in culture and deprivation.

I will have to play my part in catalysing where I can, but my main role must, of course, eventually be to make myself entirely dispensable. I am working on it.

Meanwhile, I am not a woman, I am not from a village, and I am not even African, but I do hope I get to see the tragedy of death in childbirth beginning to be a rarity in rural Tanzania.

Maybe I will.

Every dog has his day.

The Patience of Job

In Africa, life moves at a slower pace, towards an ironically shorter end. Planned change, if it happens at all, happens in African time, which begins tomorrow and then takes a break for a while. It is almost a sign of weakness to pitch up to a meeting on time in Africa, and it is certainly a sign of naivety (unless there are free sandwiches), as no one else will be there.

Even African leaders are calling for Africans to set their body clocks to today:

http://www.globaltimes.cn/content/788640.shtml

In rural Tanzania, then, those planning long-term, sustainable change, need not only all the other attributes of change agents, but also the patience of Job.

(The 'patience of Job', as you probably know, refers to the proverbial patience of an Old Testament figure who lived, it seems, soon after Abraham. He lost everything he had, including all his wealth, camels, sheep, donkeys and friends – and even his children, who all died. Then, when he had patiently proved his submission to God, he was rewarded with twice as much wealth, and twice as many camels, sheep, donkeys and friends. Also ten replacement children. These were the days before university tuition fees.)

Anyway, even Job would have raised an intolerant eyebrow at the vicissitudes of the women of rural Africa. Not dying in childbirth surely should have been an urgent need for endless generations. African women have been far too patient. Even if Job were getting restless for action, however, it does not imply that the alternative way ahead should therefore be given over entirely to *im*patience.

I say this despite being something of an expert on impatience. Surgeons are naturally impatient, but I have taken it to new levels, and indeed have invented several forms of impatience previously unknown to mankind. There cannot be many people, for instance, who never listen to the BBC news on the radio, because it is unbearable to waste six beeps of their life waiting for it to start.

My wife, by contrast, is very, very patient. When we first met, she used to slow the car as she approached green traffic lights, so as to be ready in case they turned red. Commendably safe, I am sure, but only love, deep respect, absence of dual controls, and lack of blunt instrument stopped me from taking command. Safety is not everything. I eventually brought her round by making her morning cup of tea with cold bathwater in case I scalded myself.

Anyway, here is the paradox: When things go naturally slowly, impatience can be a useful and necessary driver to kick-start some action: getting a Caesarean done quickly, for instance, in a culture where people traditionally meander to the theatre when they are ready. However, impatience is itself a blunt instrument. Getting things to happen quickly, and getting angry when they do not, is likely to produce a quick-fix solution – or drive you to an early grave without yielding a benefit.

(The early grave danger, by the way, is a particular worry, given the paroxysmal wrath induced in me by automated phone-answering systems:

"Hi! My name is Emma. Welcome to the Public Toilet Opening Times Enquiry Service.

"With my initially soothing but eventually apoplexy-inducing voice, I am going to guide you through the options, at the same time as liberally sprinkling my patronising pronouncement with infuriatingly facile irrelevancies.

"Press 1 if you would like to know the nearest public toilet to your current location. This service can only be accessed by honorary life members, or by adding the access code which you will find on the door of any public toilet.

"Press 2 if you would like to know how much time and money you have wasted on our automated phone system, and others like it, over the past year.

"Press 3 if you would like to start going round a seemingly endless set of options which eventually, by tomorrow lunchtime, leads you back to this one.

"I'm sorry. I did not understand that.

"Please try again, but without hitting your phone needlessly hard, or throwing it against a wall and stamping on the remains.

"OK. Using a six-digit number system, please say or enter on your keypad the date of birth of your favourite estate-agent's best friend.

"You seem to be having trouble.

"If you have forgotten your security data, you can refresh it now, by logging into http://www.pleaserefreshmydataeventhoughtogetonthesiteIneedmypass wordwhichI'vealsoforgotten@deathbyinternet.com, and enter the length of the second molar of your first pet.

"Well done. You are nearly there.

"Finally, while you are online, we need to know that you are not a robot. Here is a 1 cm x 1 cm picture of smudged Turkish graffiti on a toilet wall in Istanbul, in a photo taken from the International Space Station. What are the second and fourth letters of the signature?

"Press 4 if you have already been incontinent."

It's a tricky thing, then, impatience. It is not about efficiency or getting a job done as well as possible in the time available. It is not even about making sure that the final result is the one you want. Impatient driving for instance, gets you there no faster, risks not getting you there at all and annoys everyone, include yourself, in the process.

It seems to me, then, that if there is such a thing as good impatience, it is not about passion for excellence, but rather is simply about being determined that the next five seconds go to plan. Then the next five seconds, and so on. In surgery, that is almost always good. But in the rest of life, impatience is a hindrance to the smooth flowing of a calm and productive existence.

And so, finally, to the point. (Thank you for your patience.) I went out to Tanzania nearly two years ago, to the remote villages around Berega. I came back pumped up with impatient determination to help Berega tackle the desperate tragedy of death in childbirth. Out of this was born Embrace-*Tushikamane*. That project plans to begin by building a platform of women's groups in the remote rural hamlets, as we now know this to be an important prelude to success.

A year ago, we had already mustered the money to begin; the partners to help us succeed; the experts in the methodology to advise us; the charitable NGO to house our efforts; the freshly-mapped road plans of the territory; the support of the community and the hospital; the potential recruits as local project leads; three people who regularly read the blog; and even a highly-talented PhD researcher to analyse what will happen.

However, much as these achievements might have been immediately gratifying, they are not enough. On kicking off the project, we would have had a fulfilling five seconds, with many more of them to follow. But, finally, we would have joined the vast list of well-intentioned failures. The reason is this: first, we need a system whereby the women of the villages not just keep up the impetus, but spread it to surrounding villages, until it becomes the norm for rural Tanzanian women collectively to take action to tackle the roots of the problems that kill them.

Secondly, we also need successful examples of where the women's group's energy and prioritisation has led to sustainable development: better health, better nutrition, better childbirth arrangements, cleaner water, better antenatal care, better family planning and so on.

Thirdly, we need individual champions to spread the lessons. For all this to happen, and happen well, our central need is to embed the whole process in Tanzanian people, Tanzanian systems and Tanzanian ways of doing things. From the training of the project leads and community leaders, through to the coordination of responses, all of this must be integrated into a Tanzanian-led, Tanzanian-based system.

To move towards this goal, we have needed the patience of Job – and so have you, when months drift by without anything seeming to change. However, we are getting there. We have identified Ifakara as the epicentre of these developments, and we now have buy-in from two major players, each with a great international reputation for making a difference:

http://www.ihi.or.tz/ http://www.healthtrainingifakara.org/

I hope that soon we will be able to report that we have a Tanzanian project manager working with these Institutions, and a date for the start: of the collaboration, of local staff selection and of training. After far too many generations, that will be Job well done.

"Are we nearly there yet?"

When our eldest daughter was seven, the other three were aged five, three and one respectively. For holidays, we would usually pile in the car and set off for a week's camping on the continent. Long car journeys (and preparing for them), therefore, were seminars in applied child psychology:

"No, it's not an ugly plastic rucksack I found in the park, (with nothing wrong with it except a broken zip, by the way), it's a special magic fairy suitcase I borrowed from a princess!"

"Look! Dolly and Teddy are going for a wee before we set off! Does anyone else want to squeeze out a wee?"

"Eat up your food so you don't get hungry on the way. Dry bread is a special treat! Who can eat theirs first?"

"Look! Dolly and Teddy are throwing up on the roadside before we set off. Does anyone else want to get car-sick before they even get in their seats?" …

"No, not you, mummy…"

"Right! Who would like to have the special snuggly seat in the boot with all the luggage?" …

"No, not you, mummy…" etc.

However, once the journey is under way, the real psychological deal-breaker is the management of the deadly phrase, "Are we nearly there yet?" As plaintive as a baby's cry; as irritating as Kim Jong Un's haircut; and as impossible to ignore as a bevy of bickering tom-cats being struck by a falling piano. Yet ignore it you must, for the sake of your sanity. (Unless, of course, it is the driver, your saintly relative by marriage, asking "Are we nearly there yet?", after she notices that her navigator has been asleep since Milton Keynes.)

Yes, long journeys then were a real mission, full of the unexpected and, what was worse, the expected. However, what I failed to appreciate in those days of discovering that we should have turned right at France, is this: any number of factors might prevent you from spending a week in *Marais-Isolé de Mouches,* but almost all of them wreak their negative effect *before* the journey starts. By the time your car engine coughs into life, reaching the destination is almost guaranteed sooner or later. (Often later.) But, nevertheless, you arrive. It may be that you are not nearly-there-yet when you realise, after driving 50 miles, that you left

Teddy on the doorstep, but you know that, eventually, you are going to be.

And so it is that I am delighted to report that the Embrace-*Tushikamane* journey, after two years of careful planning, is finally about to begin. I wanted to say that it has been a tough two years but, in reality, it has not.

We needed first to decide how exactly we were going to tackle the awful maternal and child mortality in the rural areas served by hospitals such as Berega. As you will have gathered from foregoing chapters, when I went there for a couple of months in 2013, it was in the naïve hope of influencing the deaths in childbirth by improving the maternity services. It transpired that seven out of eight deaths occurred in the community, due to tantalisingly remediable causes, such as lack of transport when needing a Caesarean; having no money for any health intervention; lack of antibiotics in septicaemia; ruptured uterus from taking traditional medicine; lack of early recognition of blood pressure and therefore death from eclampsia; bleeding to death for lack of a simple injection to deliver the placenta etc.

This litany of awfulness would have been overwhelming had it not been for the pioneering work of Prof Anthony Costello, Mikey Rosato and the team at UCL, London. Anthony is the director of Global Health, and he and his colleagues were only too well aware that charitable interventions in utterly resource-poor settings often produced only dependency and transient benefit. They therefore devised and fine-tuned a mechanism for getting each small community to participate in determining its own destiny, beginning with setting up women's groups. Success followed success, and eventually their methodology became official WHO policy:

http://apps.who.int/iris/bitstream/10665/127939/1/9789241507271_eng.pdf?ua=1

A charity was set up to perpetuate the aims – 'Women and Children First' – and at the same time the system produced huge success in Malawi, under the leadership of Florida Banda:

http://www.maimwana.org/
https://vimeo.com/15751446

Fortunately for Embrace-*Tushikamane*, we have had enormous support from Mikey Rosato at W and C First, from Florida Banda in Malawi and from Prof Costello himself … reprising his supporting role of years ago, when he played Scrooge to my Cratchit in the school play:

"A must-see triumph! *****" (Blackheath Herald).
"Wood brought tears to my eyes" (Belmont Hill Spectator).
"I brought tears to Wood's eyes!" (My mum, when I then failed my exams).

Countless other happy coincidences (if coincidences they be) have created the circumstances for the successful start of the journey:

- the goodwill of the hospital hierarchy and the leaders of the community;
- the drive and determination of Prof Arri Coomarasamy at the University of Birmingham and the charity Ammalife, in housing the project and finding it support;
- the provision for Helen Williams to centre her PhD thesis on the project;
- the help of 'Hands4Africa' in mapping the roads;
- the support of the Diocese of Worcester and the charity Mission Morogoro for at least some of the needs which will be articulated by the women's groups;
- the generosity of many supporters in providing for the financial costs thus far;
- the free provision of materials, advice and technical support from Mikey Rosato at W and C First;
- and finally the creation of partnership with key individuals such as Dr Godfrey Mbaruku at the Ifakara Health Institute and Prof Senga Pemba at the Tanzanian Training Centre for International Health, who hope to use our project as a pilot for spreading the programme more widely in Tanzania.

Additionally, the hospital itself is getting ready for any future influx. The nursing school at the hospital has just had its registration made full instead of provisional; the paediatrician David Curnock annually visits Berega to top up skills in care of the newborn; the obstetrician Dr Ahmed Ali will be going again to Berega next month to help improve maternity services; and his wife Elizabeth, a midwife-tutor, is amidst plans to foment the engagement and training of traditional birth attendants.

However, none of this journey preparation would have been of any use without a driver, and the driver needs to be in the car, not 5,000 miles away in the UK. What a delight to report then that I think we have found the right person. He is a public health and African community project management specialist, rather than a medic, and that actually suits our purpose better.

If all goes well, he will begin his association with us by seeing how this work has already achieved a major impact in a similar setting. At the beginning of July, he will be visiting the Malawi team and villages, and will get first-hand experience of how the process works and of what it can achieve. Sometime in the autumn, when all is ready, he and I and Helen Williams will visit Berega and Tunguli, to meet the key people. We will finalise recruitment of staff, finding local champions of women's issues to begin to help the women of the villages find their voice.

And so, finally, we begin.

"Are we nearly there yet?"
Of course we are nearly there! We have set off.

From a distance

What have these three got in common?

- the Atacama Desert;
- butter beans; and
- Sir Alfred Herbert?

I'll give you a clue: this chapter, when it settles finally into its weighty purpose, will get tellingly close – too close maybe – to a very tough issue.

So: what do the Atacama, butter beans and Sir Alfred have in common? If you need more time, then look away because here is the answer: they all look better from a distance.

With the Atacama, the reason is self-evident: it is drier than binomial distribution tables, and (like the study of them), when you get stuck in it, it kills you. (I am told that, in probability theory, the binomial distribution with parameters n and p is the discrete probability distribution of the number of successes in a sequence of n independent y/n experiments, each of which yields p probability of success.

See what I mean?)

To give credit where it is due, however, the Atacama is a majestic way to dry out, but nevertheless is best appreciated from a considerably long way off.

A butter bean is the second example of something which, when experienced close up, is distinctly less palatable. Fair enough, from a distance a gang of them can look dishonestly appetising, but inadvertently bite into one of these imposters and your incisors feel like they've just got stuck into a long-abandoned mouse-nest hiding behind the lettuce. Butter beans masquerade as vegetables; they pretend to enhance good-for-you salads; they impersonate new Jersey Royal potatoes. But in fact they are nothing more than badly-packaged sawdust.

Sir Alfred Herbert is my third example of something more readily appreciable from further away. He was a 20th century Coventry philanthropist, and officer of the Belgian Order of Leopold. (In case you are wondering, I believe that the Order of Leopold was "Apportez-moi mon chocolate", but I am not sure.)

Sir Alfred donated an art gallery to Coventry, and within is the most stunning piece of art I have ever seen: the size of an entire wall, it depicts Sir Alfie by means of the most extraordinary and unlikely technique. Not only is it best seen from the other side of the gallery, but you actually need a video to take it in:

https://youtu.be/BfAW7aLayNg

Some things, then, are better appreciated from a distance.

This leads me seamlessly into the next wisp of thought-vapour emanating from the spout of my ageing kettle: "From a distance" was the title of an iconic song of my youth. Actually, I was 39 when it came out, but I felt young inside. (Funny, isn't it, how you keep on feeling 18, even when you need help putting your socks on; help hearing conversations in your garden when two bees are chatting in next-door's; help finding your glasses when someone has left them on top of your head; and help remembering who this person is who just greeted you like an old friend, but whose face is only vaguely familiar, like a book you might have read, but didn't. He's your next-door neighbour, by the way. Also ex-rugby team-mate, who shared a desk with you at work; who carried you down to base-camp when you broke your leg on Everest; married your sister; and is godfather to three of your children. But normally he wears glasses.)

Anyway, "From a distance" was the title of an iconic song of my youth. There's a bit in it that goes:

"From a distance,
"We are instruments
"Marching in a common band,
"Playing songs of hope,
"Playing songs of peace,
"They are the songs of every man."

For a generation of baby boomers, brought up on 'love, not war', this struck a beautiful and harmonious chord. We really did feel the hope and the peace.

But what, I now wonder, did the song mean by "from a distance"? Did it mean from far away in space? In time? In perception? Surely it did not mean that, from a distance, there was hope and peace, but when you got right up close, it turned out that there was just corruption and irreconcilable intolerance?

I don't think so. Of course, corruption and intolerance are with us always, and you will always stumble over them when trying to influence any of the world's crises. But I think perhaps that the song was saying this: there is such a thing as being too close to a problem. You only see the day-to-day frustrations; the two steps back, not the three steps forward; the fly, not the ointment; the one curmudgeon, not the 100 supporters; the broken parachute, not the lovely view. (Note to self: need to work on the metaphors.)

From a distance, in other words, you can see how far we have come, rather than only how far left to go. So, from a distance, the Embrace-*Tushikamane* project has grown from being a shy skinny infant of a project, to a well-balanced healthy youngster, ready to leave home and set the world to rights. From a distance, we have come a long way – as chronicled in this book and summarised in the post:

http://yellowchuckchucks.blogspot.co.uk/2015/07/tushikamane-we-are-in-solidarity.html

However, if there is such a thing as being too close to a problem, there is also such a thing as being too far away. Last week, five thousand miles away in Dar es Salaam, our new Tanzanian project leader was due to activate his role, with the objective of having five 'community participation' groups up and running by next Easter. A short time into the job, he has resigned.

From close up, this is a disaster. Who will run the project now? A central point at issue, however, was what to do about the status quo encountered in many African schemes: corruption. The project leader's proposal included the payment of 'thank-you' sums to village leaders, to incentivise them to allow us into the village. Yes, really. To allow us to help them reduce maternal and child death.

Should we bribe village leaders to allow us to help bring the village into the 21st century? No! This is not the way to lead under-resourced people into a better world. Of course, I understand that corruption not only exists, but is deeply embedded in many countries. I know that fighting it at high level is a thankless, though not hopeless, task. However, although it might be naïve to believe it, we are on the cusp of something new and fresh: the empowerment of women in rural impoverished communities, with the sure knowledge that this leads to betterment of village life at every level.

We have been privileged to be party to the World Health Organisation's most modern strategy for preventing the tragic loss of mothers and children. We have been presented with all their materials and methodology. Now we are going to make it happen. Corrupt back-handers to traditional village leaders are not part of this vision and, I firmly hope, will not only be rejected by those organising the support of the communities, but also by the communities themselves.

We have a plan B, and even as I write this, the Berega and Tunguli communities themselves are coming up with a responsible and sustainable strategy, which does not include 'incentives'. More of this in the next chapter, I hope.

Managing the process from 5,000 miles away has the advantage of allowing me not to be over-disconcerted by setbacks. I can see where we are going, and I know all too well how bad the problems were before we began the journey. Going back is not an option.

However, what we also need now, besides the vision and direction, is the right people in the right roles. Close to the heart of the problems, we need Tanzanians who take a dogged and courageous pride in what we hope to achieve. Rural Africans who are determined that the villages will leave far behind them both the tragedy and corruption of days gone by.

Maybe their children will look back, from a distance, and feel the warm glow expressed by a song they never heard, but maybe always knew:

"From a distance, there is harmony, and it echoes through the land. It's the voice of hope, it's the voice of peace, it's the voice of every man."

Yearning for life

How do we change bad situations? Why is it so tough to tackle sustainable development goals, even when everyone seems on the same side? Allow me a little diversion to illustrate the difficulty … then persevere through the serious bits, because the conclusion not only illustrates why the women's group 'Tushikamane' project is necessary, but casts an explanatory beam or two on how we might make Earth a better planet.

But to begin with the diversion: Common chicory is a woody perennial found on the roadsides of Europe. Being one of the few roadside plants which is not poisonous to humans, it has found its way in various forms into our diet in times of need. In times of positively desperate need, in fact, because it tastes like a woody perennial found on roadsides.

One such time of desperate need was in 1876 in India, when Gordon Highlanders sat around the camp fire gagging for a nice cup of wet after a hard day's colonising. Coffee was more popular than tea in the Victorian era, but coffee in the military field of combat was not to be had. Victorian Britain may have had plenty of colonies that produced the bean, but they also had plenty of other fields of combat, as they endeavoured to subsume the Canadians, Afghans, Chinese, Sikhs, Maoris, Hottentots, Ashantis, Zulus, Egyptians, Sudanese, Boers, Mexicans, Malays, Australian Aborigines, Caucasians, Ugandans, Tanganyikans, Persians, Bolivians, Nagas, Abyssinians, Burmese, Greeks, Crimeans, Japanese, West Africans, Ceylonese, Somalis, and of course, the Irish.

Then someone back home in Scotland had the brilliantly parsimonious idea to add chicory to coffee to bulk it out – or, to be more precise, to add a tiny touch of coffee to chicory. The resulting brew is called Camp, and has been popular in every war ever since. Indeed, for many, it continued to be the chosen stimulant right up until the end of rationing in 1954.

Here's the rub: my mum was brought up on the stuff, and so you would have thought that she would dream of the day when she could get an extra-hot, skinny-latte whenever the whim took her. Not so. Camp carried on being her tipple for another five decades after proper coffee became available. Why? Why do people carry on doing what they have always done, even when it includes drinking something that looks and tastes like mud?

Is the answer that awfulness can be preferable to possibility? Or rather, that comfortable, predictable, secure, stable, in-your-control, familiar awfulness is more appealing to the human condition than uncomfortable, unpredictable, insecure, unstable, out-of-your-control, unfamiliar possibility?

Is this really true? If you do not like philosophy, you can stop reading now, but if you do, then get yourself a *grande cappuccino*, a comfy seat on an old leather sofa, an exorbitantly-priced two-centimetre-square piece of flapjack made of three seeds and a sultana, and read my take on this fundamentally vital topic.

Imagine a bubble village, where each house represents one of us: For most of us, we make the inside of our bubble comfortable, predictable, secure, stable and in-our-control. Indeed, so strong are these instincts that we persuade ourselves that everything within the bubble is as it should be. Self-deception is at the heart of obstinacy. In this process, knowledge and reason are laid carefully in a bottom drawer, to be accessed only when called for. (We commonly use reason, not to modify what we want or believe, but to justify it.) The internal environment of our bubble may not be healthy, but we get used to it. We develop habits. We grow accustomed. We do what we always did. And we pretend to ourselves that this is how things should be.

Then someone tries to break into our bubble – to persuade us, for instance, to stop smoking; to eat less cholesterol; to be nice to people we don't like; to exercise more; to be more client-friendly; to be more spiritual; to be less traditionalist; and to be more reliable when told to buy some more bread next day, even when she only told you in passing at midnight when you'd already had two glasses of wine (and anyway why didn't she buy the bread when she was at the shops herself that very day?)

Of course then, when someone tries to break into your house, you bolt the boor, bar the windows and hide behind the settee. So many or even most of us live in our cosy bubble.

Others of us, (the more enlightened, or the more annoying?), spend most of the time out of our own cocoon, pestering people, by trying to break into theirs. Giving unwanted information is simply nagging;

unwanted rationalisation is spurious; unwanted help is imposition; and unwanted instruction is oppression.

To make the whole situation more complicated, the entire bubble-village is itself within a bubble, and what applies singly to the individual also applies collectively to the community and the culture. The bubble-villagers like things just the way they are, thank you.

The truly enlightened, then, not only do not obstinately stay within their own bubble, but do not even stay within their own village of bubbles. They will be on the outside, exhausting themselves going from village to village, bashing their ideas on the outer walls. (Oscar Wilde was one such wanderer, whose quote "Whenever people agree with me, I always feel I must be wrong", laid the foundation for 21st century democracy.)

(By the way, it must have been a nightmare living with someone who only talks in quotes:

You: "Good morning, Oscar. Cup of tea?"
Him: "I can resist everything except temptation!"
You: "So is that a yes?"
Him: "Selfishness is not living as one wishes to live, it is asking others to live as one wishes to live."
You: "So you do want one, then?"
Him: "I have the simplest tastes. I am always satisfied with the best."
You: "So you mean you want a cup?"
Him: "There are only two tragedies in life: one is not getting what one wants, and the other is getting it."
You: "I can't stand this! I'm going to make myself a cup of tea."
Him: "True friends stab you in the front."
You: "I'm off."
Him: "Some cause happiness wherever they go; others whenever they go.")

Anyway, where were we? Oh yes! Let's come down with a bump back into musing on what makes people resist change.

Collective normality, it seems, is the ultimate determinant of our behaviour and, within those collective norms, we mainly sit in our bubbles and make our own delusions. And so it is that if a plane crashes in Russia with no survivors; or a tsunami kills a quarter of a million people; or your next-door neighbour develops aggressive cancer; or you develop chronic bronchitis; or you get put in prison with a tolerable enough room-mate; or the planet slowly overheats; or your country goes to war; or someone's sister bleeds to death in childbirth on the floor of a mud-hut, that life goes on. You have your cuppa and watch Coronation Street on Wednesdays.

It should not be surprising, then, that change is so hard: to change the way things are, you have to change people. But you cannot change people – we can only change ourselves. We have to take the chain off the door of the cocoon, have a peep outside, be lured to step out into uncertain reality ... and to become someone slightly different. We have to lose a bit of ourselves, and that is scary.

What might lure us to do this? To change not just that with which we are familiar, but actually to change something of who we are? Information, reasons, instructions are not enough. In fact, they can simply be intrusive. To get people to do something as radical as embrace change, things have to be yearned for. Indeed, I could go so far as to say this: without actual yearning, no sustainable change is possible.

We cannot just tell people what they need. We cannot just pitch up with our ready-made solutions. Our stock-in-trade must be questions, rather than answers. We must listen. And to do this, we must give a voice to those who most need it – the women and children of remote villages for whom the death toll of life is so high. Such women have become accustomed to the normality of awfulness. They may feel powerless in the face of the weary blocks that impede sustained development: inertia, opposition, vested interest, self-interest, partisan groups, intolerance, corruption, resentment and ambition. All of these, however, relate to the collective mentality, and when that collective thinking is a yearning for things to be different, then they will be.

And so to *Tushikamane*, the project which is trying to reduce the tragic deaths of mothers and babies in the villages of Tunguli, in rural Tanzania. This month, the *Tushikamane* team leaders are visiting the MaiMwana project, to experience amazing examples of this collective determination in action.

http://vimeo.com/12427420
http://www.maimwana.org/

Later in the month I will be going out to Tunguli, to be involved in the final week of team training. Thereafter, the team will begin the process of mobilising community participation and women's voices in each of six hamlets deep in the Tanzanian bush.

Working from the manuals and materials kindly supplied by Women and Children First, we have produced a full set of materials, and have translated the key ones into Swahili for use by our front-line staff. All these resources are now posted on a *Tushikamane* blog. For those who like detail, they give a blow-by-blow account of how *Tushikamane* intends to reduce death of mothers and babies.

http://yellowchuckchucks.blogspot.co.uk/

The bottom line is this: telling people what to do does not produce sustainable change. Even if the people are asking "Why must we do it?", it means that they are still in the cocoon.

When they are asking "How can we do it?", however, and yearning for the answer, it means that they are on the way to a new destiny and, for some, a new life.

Yes, yearning for life. That is what we need.

Thanksgiving

Thanksgiving originally began with Michaelmas, at the end of September. In fact, for the Celts, the entire year began with Michaelmas. Punctuated by the quarterly pagan festivals of yule, easter and midsummer, the Druidic year finally wound up with a thanksgiving for the harvest. Along with thanksgiving, the end of the Celtic year was traditionally a time for the settling of debts, the renewing of employment and, apocryphally, the sacking of the manager if they had lost to Rangers.

American Thanksgiving, then, as a celebration, had its roots in the Autumnal Equinox Celtic harvest festival. The pilgrim survivors of the Mayflower in 1621, however, had to wait until the end of November for there to be enough provender on the table, and enough turkeys stupid enough to wonder what the business end of a blunderbuss smelt like.

Each year thereafter, the pilgrims gave thanks.

And so it was that the custom grew up in the New World that, on a Thursday in late November, entire extended families of turkeys would gather together in WalMart, having been persuaded that they would thereby be first in line for Black Friday Christmas bargains. (Thursdays have since been generally considered by turkeys as unlucky, as have sage, cranberries, Bacofoil and ovens.)

The reason for this educational and historically insightful introduction is that a recent Thursday was indeed, for many, Thanksgiving Day, and I was invited to my first ever Thanksgiving dinner. The setting was the staff house at Berega Mission Hospital in rural Morogoro, Tanzania.

http://www.youtube.com/watch?v=n84o3Mztf9o

Several of the surrounding houses are home to some wonderful American 'Hands4Africa' volunteers, who teach at the local village school. (The selfless determination and drive of Brad Logan, Ruth Mgego and H4A supporters have, in five short years, developed the school exponentially. From a hut in which the legendary Mama Liz taught six sparky kids, it has become a set of inspiringly embellished classes catering for more than 130 eager and successful local village pupils. What joy to see the next generation of Tanzanians being disabused of a heritage of poverty and ignorance.)

Thanksgiving Day itself, coincidentally, was the last day of the school year, and so teachers Lisa, Marianne, Bette and Chris were ready and eager for a night of shared festivity. Dr Kristien, Dr Al and his wife engineer Emma made up the rest of the gang, along with my good self. The fayre was classic Berega: stone-ground bread (ie bread made from ground stones); chopped tomato and onion with amoebic dressing; micro-omelette from local pygmy chickens; goats'-nest soup; marsh cactus wedges; and of course the traditional 'brown-crunch' – a sort of vegetarian version of dung beetle.

We ate. We drank a little beer. We put the world to rights. We killed a few cockroaches (although somewhat pointlessly. Others sprang into the breach to take their place, climbing over injured comrades to sell their lives dearly.) And then we sang. Lisa has a heavenly voice somewhere between Joni Mitchell and Lady Gaga. She said that my voice was somewhere between Elvis and Pavarotti, but it turns out she meant geographically, reminding her of a traumatic bird-watching experience in the Azores.

One telling moment was when each of us had to say something we were especially grateful for in the last year. Having had a new granddaughter in May, my special thanks was for offspring. Thinking back, it strikes me now that the thanksgiving contribution of each of the others was just a sentence or two, so perhaps I shouldn't have shown quite so many photos of my youngest granddaughter, Layla Miriam.

("This is Layla lying on a mat. Here she is lying on a different mat. This one is of her looking quizzical at the mat change. She's very intelligent, you know. She can tell the difference between presbyopia and hyperopia, often taking the glasses from my face when I'm not reading. Here's another one of her not on any mat at all ... " etc)

At about midnight, Kristien went off to check the hospital, and so ended a lovely first Thanksgiving. A quick cull of mini-predators, a sluice of the torso with a moist banana leaf, and I was deeply asleep. Somewhere before dawn, I was woken by what at first seemed like singing, coming from the distance and getting louder and louder. As it passed nearer the house, I could hear that it was wailing: a heart-rending, plaintive, inconsolable wailing that I knew meant death. I got up, but what could I do? So I went back to a troubled sleep.

Next morning, Kristien was up before seven, despite her nocturnal tribulations. She told me that when she arrived at the hospital, she found them unsuccessfully trying to resuscitate a four-year-old boy, who was dying of cholera. His brother was also badly dehydrated, and the father less so, but both still very ill, pooing and vomiting uncontrollably. The wailing, then, was for the death of the young lad? No, said Kristien, it was for a pregnant woman at full term, who died at the hospital gates from a ruptured uterus. Maybe fear of the rain kept her too long at home, or maybe it was fear of upsetting the traditional birth attendant, or fear of the cost of hospital, or fear of dying there. Most likely a combination of fears, some well-founded.

So a death of a mother and of her baby and a further child death, all in a day? Not only, said Kristien. Yet another baby died in the premature baby room, and yet another again was on the brink when she went to bed.

I said poignant goodbyes and set off for Dar es Salaam without knowing what happened to the father and son. This is a video of what the terrain looked like along the way and, between poverty and lack of infrastructure, you can see why death is so desperately common:

https://youtu.be/aJuhyV2oOBg

Kristien will have been in the hospital for the best part of a year when she leaves before Christmas: home to Belgium and family and friends, and winter and jumpers and comfort and showers and toilets and food; and chocolate; and sprouts; and safe refuge from cockroaches, cholera and unending tragedy. An amazing woman. Interestingly, when I asked her how she had coped with so much, it was Thanksgiving in a way that kept her sanity. Ranting about the fickleness of fate leads to anger, and anger erodes. It's knowing that sometimes you make a difference that keeps you going – sometimes, thankfully, but only sometimes.

But in my Thanksgiving week at Berega, there was indeed something important to be thankful for. The Embrace / *Tushikamane* project was officially launched, and the *Tushikamane* team took the helm.

Chairman is Rev Isaac Mgego, who is also director of the hospital. He is a man of God and a man of the people, having been the first person in his village to go beyond primary education. He paid for it himself by making and selling charcoal, and eventually finished his education with an MBA. His will visit the project villages weekly, with the project director, Wilbard Mrase. His role will be to help solve high-level issues, and to make bridges to other initiatives and organisations working to the same end.

Wilbard Mrase is the powerhouse who will teach, drive, direct, fix, make things happen – and report back monthly the progress and problems. His day job is to lead the Berega school of nursing, and his passion is reduction of maternal death in the community.

Rev Dr Alex Gongwe is a charismatic medic living within, and serving, the Tunguli and Msamvu communities. Here he is, role-playing with facilitators Simon and Esther, showing how not to persuade villagers to improve their lot:

https://youtu.be/tHWwrpdVehk

He is the project supervisor, and is the direct boss of the front-line workers. His role is to equip them with the skills, materials and understanding they will need for each micro-stage of the journey; to listen; to trouble-shoot; to fix things; to expect appropriate activity; and to help turn activity into achievement ... and measurement of achievement. He will also look for synergies and harmonies, not just between the facilitators, but also between *Tushikamane* and other village-level initiatives.

The facilitators are Esther Paul, Noadia Mganga and her assistant, Simon Jackson. They will be the ones going into the hamlets, meeting the young women, the pregnant women, the mothers and the female influencers. They will begin a chain of events whereby they listen to the women's voices, and they muster their collective yearning for things to be different. The vital ingredient of the process is that the village women themselves probe what might be the roots of the staggering death rates of mothers and children. The village women themselves then prioritise which three or four of these they would like to tackle, with the help of the men. The *Tushikamane* team will help them align to any useful support, initiatives and organisations.

But even with a good idea such as community-participation-with-the-aim-of-reducing-death, you can't just pitch up and get on with it. In Africa especially, you need buy-in at every level, and you need the imprimatur of the powers-that-be. And so it was that Wilbard and Isaac called an introductory meeting of the entire superstructure of the Tunguli and Msamvu villages.

Quite incredibly, no fewer than 37 headmen, leading women, teachers, elders, priests, imams, health workers, NGO workers and the like, gathered for what was in effect the local launch of *Tushikamane*. Oh yes, and me. A three-hour discussion in Swahili ensued, some of which I did not follow. (Specifically, the bit after "Good morning, ladies and gentlemen ...") It worked. The response of the (mainly male) community leaders was not just overwhelming support (deeply encouraging though that was), it was that they really understood where we were coming from. One by one, they got up to say so. Change had to come from within. Sustainable change to maternal mortality had to start with mothers.

They got it.

As I began to write this from a comfortable hotel in Dar es Salaam, the week in Berega seemed almost unreal. Just 350 kilometers away from Dar, death is a frequent visitor to every village, and yet here, I had just had a door-knock from the hotel anti-pest service, offering to spray my curtains with anti-mosquito. (I asked if they could spray the door with anti-knock, but they did a runner.) Soon, I would be at home with a glass of vino in one hand, and metaphor in the other, putting the final touches to this chapter, from the comfort of Earlsdon.

Like the Pilgrim Fathers, I feel that I have so much to be thankful for. Maybe this Christmas, as you peel the Bacofoil from the unlucky bird, you might want to give a thankful thought for how far much of the world has come since those pioneers ... and a wistful one for how far much of it still has to go.

Expecting mothers ...

When I first started going out with my lovely wife, we discovered unexpected things about each other. Once we got beyond the unbridled physical passion (on my part anyway; hers was more an unbridled physical forbearance), we each realised that our new sweetheart had certain annoying attributes which needed fixing. As you might imagine, mine are still being fixed. Wives have an uncanny talent for fine-tuning the end marital product.

By contrast, I was almost completely happy with the product I was getting, and indeed a short while into the relationship, I tore up the receipt.

There was one thing about my beautiful inamorata, however, that drove me potty: patience. It is an attribute that I have had cause to mention before in this book, and I hope you will bear with me if I reprise the subject. But, I hear you say:

"Patience? But that is a worthy and desirable characteristic in a person, surely?"
And you would be right ... up to a point.

"Up to a point? A point where impatience is better than calm equipoise? Surely not?", I hear you add.

(I will be OK from here on in, by the way, if you want to take a break from interrupting people's writing.)

Yes, there is indeed a point where impatience is better than calm equipoise. And, as I have already explained, it is this: green traffic lights. Who in their right mind (other than my wife-to-be) slows down at green traffic lights 'in case they turn red'? What sort of mad sealing-of-one's-own-fate is that? Of course they might turn red. That is what they do! They are traffic lights, for pity's sake! We are already being overtaken by octogenarians recovering from hip surgery, so yes, they will indeed be red by the time we get there! We cannot spend the rest of our lives together stopping at both red and green traffic lights!

Anyway, you get the point. Miriam is a naturally patient person, and I am not (although I am considerably better for the four decades of uxorial effort put into upgrading me).

(Before moving on, by the way, let me just point out that natural impatience is not, in itself, a vice. It has, occasionally, stood me in good stead – for instance in surgical crises, where the stop-at-green equivalent might be

"Hi everyone! How are things? And the family? Oh my, Bernie! Is that green you are wearing?! It's funky, man!! It was great fun last Friday, wasn't it? Do you know, sometimes we should just take deep breaths and suck in the pure joy of our friendship.

But not now, because I just cut the aorta by mistake."

I freely admit that this is a wildly inappropriate stereotype of patient people, and that they are almost always right. And that patience even in surgery is a key attribute. I just needed to get it off my chest.)

Funnily enough, however, as I have previously pointed out, something within impatience does have another, positive and somewhat more unlikely role. I am referring to a role in Africa, where patience is traditionally measured on a different spectrum (archetypally, where 'never' is only just above mid-point). To be impatient in an African project is to self-explode. Indeed, if you look carefully in the bush around where you intend your project to take place, you might well find the spleen of a predecessor who had a similar idea.

Why, then, am I feeling a bit sanguine at my choleric disposition? Well, it seems that when you strip away the negative aspects of impatience – the bad vibes; the intolerance; the jumping to conclusions; the making mistakes; – you are left with something actually pretty useful: expectation. The expectation that, at the right time, the right thing will happen. (A bit like preparing a crab for the table: when you take off the bits that pinch you and the bits that poison you, there is something worth having inside, if you are fond of crab.)

This type of expectation is not vague or misty. It knows what it is after, knows it is coming and is waiting, bright-eyed and alert, for it to arrive. It is not to be denied.

The setting up of *Tushikamane* took two-and-a-half years, and demanded, not just patience, but a type of steadfast, quiet determination on behalf of many people, at which I, for my part, was not very good. But now, we have begun. The teams are trained; equipped; locally commissioned; accepted. They have now entered the small collections of mud-huts in distant Tunguli and Msamvu, and have begun to form women's groups. These groups will be taken through a process whereby they explore the roots of the problems that kill them and their children. Thereafter, it will be the women themselves who lead the process of prioritising which problems each hamlet is going to tackle.

Here is an excerpt from the February report of Wilbard Mrase, the project director:

"*Tushikamane* project is progressing well; already three women's groups are formed at Kwiboma in Tunguli and Dibabala and Kipera in Msamvu village. Each group has a chairperson and a secretary.

"Kwimboma has 18 women in the group, and the group is called *Amani* (which means 'peace'). Dibalala has 30 women in the group, and group is called *Upendo* (which means 'love). Kipera has 18 women in the group, and name of the group not yet given. These three hamlets Kwiboma, Dibabala and Kipera decided/agreed to meet every Saturday at 2pm, Sunday at 2pm and Friday at 9am respectively every week.

"On 27th and 28th January we will be in Tunguli and Msamvu in order to facilitate establishment of another four women's groups (two groups in each village)."

So it's happening. We have women's groups in remote villages in Tanzania where 10% of children die and maternal death is a frequent visitor. The expecting mothers for the first time will have an empowered and legitimate voice in determining what to what to do about these tragedies.

And we also have an expectation, an impatience: to consign these avoidable deaths to history.

Photosynthesis

When I was 12, plants and their products (with a few exceptions) did not impress me: I hated beans and greens; I ignored flowers in bowers; I avoided rooms with blooms. Gardens were for playing in. I liked climbable trees, apples and piles of dead leaves. I was an autumnal boy.

It was my lovely wife who first pointed out spring. She did so during 'country walks', an activity utterly foreign to someone who had grown up on the streets and spaces of south-east London. Country walks, (in case you are not familiar with the concept), are where you deliberately set off on foot to where there are no pavements, no shops, no ball games and no listless gangs of youths; and you keep going until you get back to where you started. They are not, however, totally pointless, if your wife or girlfriend is a lover of nature, as every so often she will delightedly point at a darting flash of colour above a bubbling beck and say "Ooh look, a lesser-spotted dog-eagle!" Or will tiptoe up to a fragrant cluster of common-goat's-frog pygmy-orchid, and ecstatically point out a painted-tortoise-brim fritillary caught in the very act of dipping its nose into the nectar.

You may think that these species-names are exotic, but that is what she told you they were called, and you believed her. When your wife-to-be recognises that you know nothing of birds, plants, butterflies or spring, she is at liberty to invent exotic names for anything you might encounter: "Don't tread on that, it's marsh-toadflax-lady's-beard-wort!" etc.) Inevitably, these experiences enhance the mystique, both of your loved one, and of her colourful world. And so it is, 40-odd years later, that I also have learned to rejoice in the glorious reincarnation wrought by Spring.

In February, the earth is brown and the air is grey, wet and cold. Then, impossibly, Mother Earth rolls up her sleeves and gets to work. New leaves poke out from the ground; buds peep out from the twigs; funds pop out from the bank account. (It's not all good.) One day, at a pre-arranged dawn signal before the humans are awake, yellow banks of daffodils surreptitiously rush in and swap places with their unripe brothers and sisters. The first bank to burn bright yellow sends a signal to the next, like Gondor sending a message to Rohan. Within a week or two, every roadside is sprinkled with yellow. Other flowers, embarrassed to have been pre-empted by the daffs yet again, then start falling over themselves to burst into blossom, and to paint countryside and gardens a riot of colour.

What, you might be asking, has this got to do with forming women's groups in rural Tanzania (with a view to reducing tragic death)? Good point. Well, the answer is this: photosynthesis. When a gardener gets out her spade and fork in March to encourage spring to get things moving, she is not relying only on her own efforts, but also on some immense and unseen power which she hopes to harness. She does a bit of spadework. She adds some lowly compost. She maybe sows a frugal seedling or two.

(In our garden, she would have to add a few other tasks:

- Raking up a five-foot snow-drift of leaves which have blown into the corner of the patio, obscuring the garden table and chairs which left you, throughout winter, with a horror that there might still be a guest from your last autumn barbecue lost underneath;
- Removing from the 'lawn': the children's broken bike; the deflated football; your grandson's special stick; your other grandson's special stick; a random broken piece of plastic; your best gardening glove, (the other one of which you will find after you have thrown this one away); a garden chair with three legs; and a non-matching garden chair leg, all of which you've been meaning to deal with since September.
- Putting down some lawn seed for the pigeons;
- Pulling up the clumps of the particularly hardy variety of grass that grows everywhere except the 'lawn'; and, finally
- Giving the weeds their own space, in the hope that this might appease them.)

Anyway, these pre-spring tasks achieved, the gardener then steps back and waits. Invisibly, light checks with heat to see if heat is ready. Heat has a word with water. When the three of them are set, the seemingly magical transformation sets in. Goodness pumps into root and leaf; strong and good things grow; fruit develops.

In nature, photosynthesis is at the heart of the annual extravaganza: making life from light itself. Seeing how photosynthesis helps turn the brown earth into flower and fruit and fertility, made me think about other examples of where goodness materialises as a result of harnessing the power that was always there: community spirit in a crisis; charity efforts that blossom unexpectedly; youth and sport leaders bringing out the best in youngsters; friends rallying round a friend in need; and, on a big scale (one for ageing hippies like me), when the Vietnam War looked like going on for ever, 'Make Love, Not War' stopped it. The right people plus the right conditions, and good things happen.

In the past, when charities 'did things' to disadvantaged communities, they were surprised when progress slowly got clogged and static. They did not understand the need to mobilise the energy and determination of those they were trying to help. *Tushikamane* represents a better way of working, whereby the actual starting point is such community mobilisation and empowerment. The right people plus the right conditions, and solutions emerge.

In *Tushikamane*, 11 women's groups have begun the process of harnessing this hidden potential. We now have 11 seedlings, one in each of 11 isolated hamlets in rural Tunguli and Msamvu. By July, we hope that all 11 will be strong, hardy and deeply rooted, ready to produce good fruit. The gardeners are working hard and, so far, the response is heartening.

There is a power all around us, without which nothing can be. When the right circumstances come together, the power is harnessed. Whether you believe this to be the power of God, or the power of Nature, or the power within us, the reality is that there is much good waiting to be unleashed; waiting for the circumstances; waiting to make new harmonies.

Waiting for spring.

June Drop

In the last chapter, I wrote about the 11 new women's groups which have been set up in rural Tanzania, in and around the villages of Msamvu and Tunguli.

The road to Tunguli

This territory has particular need: up-country from the inland town of Morogoro, it regularly gets cut off by the rivers, which become raging torrents in the rainy months. There are only dirt roads, shredded by the seasonal water into potholes and ruts. No villagers have cars, but a few who can afford it own or share a motorbike, in the hope rather than the expectation that these cheaply-made machines can safely make the long bumpy journeys to market or hospital.

It's ironic, in a part of the world where water creates such problems, that its absence is even more troublesome. In the small health centre in central Tunguli, water is collected from the roof. For most villagers in the surrounding remote and inaccessible tracts of land, however, the daily task of fetching this unreliable friend falls to the girls and the women. Speaking of the scarcity of water, please allow me a diversion.

I am writing this from the *Gare du Nord* in Paris, where Starbucks have just charged me a week's wages for a thimbleful of organically-sourced skinny eau with an extra shot. And it's raining. If I didn't like the French, I could have achieved the same effect more cheaply by standing on the pavement with my tongue out.

When so many are thirsty for this precious resource, but cannot afford the infrastructure, how did it come about that we fortunate few are happy to pay top dollar for plastic-encased beads of moisture? I suppose that we just got used to it, like we got used to urban foxes; having to remember your first pet's maiden name; middle-aged cyclists looking cool in bulging yellow Lycra; Whats-Apping your kids to say breakfast's ready; buying a conservatory in Lidl when you only went in for a sandwich; estate agents; and Donald Trump's hair.

But where will it lead, this capacity of ours to normalise the unfamiliar and even the bizarre? Our meek acquiescence, for instance, drip by drip and drop for drop, to pay more for rain than for milk? I imagine a conversation in Starbucks, a generation hence:

Me: Good morning!
Robot: Good morning, surprisingly-not-yet-dead Laurence Wood of Bide-a-Wee Incontinence Village, whose recent online purchases lead me to infer that you may not yet be a dedicated Galaxybucks customer. How can I help you today?
Me: I'd like a grande aero-cino with an extra breath, please.
Robot: Would you like that at normal lung humidity or extra-moist?
Me: Ummm ... normal humidity but helium enhanced, please. I need a lift ...
Robot: LOL, sir. Would you like a gluten-free, lactose-free, nut-free, fat-free, calorie-free, bee-free snack to go with that, sir? I'd recommend a raisin, or an oat.
Me: Actually, I still haven't had my 16-a-day, so I'd better go with the virtual orange pip ... Oh yes, and also, do you have a cold hand-wash?
Robot: A frappo-cleano? Certainly, sir. How will you be paying? Mortgage or krugerrand?

Of course I will be lucky to be alive a generation hence, to witness this scenario. (My wife, looking over my shoulder, says she will be lucky if I'm not.)

Anyway, in rural Tanzania, ironically cheap water washes away the soil and the roads, and infected water kills the vulnerable. On the other hand, lack of water is at the root both of poverty and of its perpetuation. Girls have to miss school in order to collect it, from the moment that they can carry a Starbuck-ful on their heads. For many girls in this part of Africa, even if there were a school, they could not attend, because essential household duties interpose themselves in the difficult business of staying alive.

And staying alive can indeed be hard. Nearly 1% of mothers die of pregnancy-related causes, and 10% of children do not reach their fifth birthday. Few earn $2 per day, and most subsist on porridge, plus what they can grow in the unforgiving terrain.

Water problems; poverty; malnutrition; poor transport; no crops; inadequate education; unaffordable, inaccessible childbirth facilities. These are some of the root-causes of tragic death that we anticipate might be highlighted in the current discussions in the 11 women's groups in Tunguli and Msamvu. Thereafter, we hope that the communities, now motivated and focused, might begin long-term sustainable projects to tackle these desperate issues.

But will it work? Will this protracted and meticulous process really arouse the community buy-in we are looking for, whereby village women truly get to grips with the root causes of tragedy, and truly determine, with our help or without it, to make a difference? Well, the WHO says yes, it will work and women will feel empowered; and yes, it is indeed the only way to progress.

But are we missing something? ...

I am now writing this from a pool-side paradise on the island of Elba, a glorious fragment of Tuscany carelessly dropped in the sea when they were making Italy. From where I lounge in the perfect, tingling Italian sun, I can see a host of fruit trees laden with lemons, oranges, avocados, bananas, figs and those little apricot-coloured ones that aren't kumquats. (Apricots?)

At the feet of these healthy, fecund trees is the 'June drop': in June, a portion of the fruit falls to the ground to leave room for the rest to flourish. This is nature's thinning-out of the crop, to enhance the abundance of the fruiting. At the right time and with the right help, these mature trees, that began as thin seedlings, will yield rich harvests.

So it will be, perhaps, with the 11 women's groups. They began as fragile plants; barely seedlings: full of the right DNA, but thin and vulnerable. Maybe not all will reach the same maturity. Maybe some of the projects which emerge will drop early to the ground.

But far from fretting that each fall represents failure of the whole, the important thing is to know that the groups are there, being tended: an orchard of possibility where before there was hunger. Yes, we are indeed on the right lines.

Water is a case in point. In the past, there have been many examples of water projects failing because they were not initiated by those in need. Good people with kind hearts decided perhaps that a village needed water, and paid for a spring or a well. Even if these sponsors managed to avoid the common problem of some of the money disappearing and managed to ensure that the rest was well-spent and managed to supervise the project so that good materials were used and were well-engineered, all of this still falls short of having ensured that lives will be saved, and that girls will be educated. See this link for the sobering facts:

http://www.vossfoundation.org/assets/www.rural-water-supply.net_.pdf

Foreign aid cannot be there for ever, maintaining the equipment; dealing with standing water; protecting from infection; encouraging appropriate use; building on success by incorporating new ideas, such as food gardens; changing the culture; and redeploying well the countless hours previously spent by women and girls in collecting this wonderful resource. When, on the other hand, a village has determined that its objective is to reduce tragic death, if it then decides that access to clean water is part of the solution, it will not put up with poor construction, poor maintenance or stasis in the primitive culture of subsistence, helplessness and tolerance of tragedy.

May I finish with a true story that was one of the reasons *Tushikamane* began?

We have six weeks to go until Canon John Green leads a party from Worcestershire to visit Tunguli and Msamvu. They will get a feel for whether the groups are really going to work, and whether some of them – hopefully most of them – have truly got to grips with what they plan to do to move towards the 21st century.

It was John Green who encouraged me, exactly three years ago, to go to Berega, to try to help prevent maternal death, by improving standards in the hospital. I knew in theory that more than 80% of deaths occurred in the community and never reached our doors, but I thought that my presence in the maternity ward would at least help. Then, one awful Saturday night in June, a woman was brought in, the middle passenger on a motor-bike, dying of complications of pregnancy. She barely had time to reach a bed before she died. To my indescribable horror, she was then loaded back onto the motorbike, again as a middle passenger, and taken back to her grieving children. The unutterable awfulness of their joy turning to grief, when they realised that the returning mother was dead, still haunts me now.

I do not know what she died of, but there are so many ways in which a determined community might have prevented her death with simple interventions: training of birth attendants not to give stimulants; early transport systems; iron to treat anaemia in pregnancy such that any bleeding does not kill you; early detection of pre-eclampsia; clean water and cleanliness to prevent infection; the list of interventions is long, and the list of common killers is short. The story is similar and 10 times as common for deaths of under-fives, where clean water is a huge part of the solution.

We begin with 11 women's groups. Maybe some of the groups will not be as strong as others. Maybe some will even fail - the June drop of human enterprise.

But if they prevent just one June drop of that more horrific kind, then *Tushikamane* will have succeeded.

Brexiting

As I began to write this, Britain was going to the polls to decide whether to remain in the EU, or whether to 'Brexit' – to leave the European Union. I was not really deeply acquainted with the arguments, despite having heard the spin, seen the posters and drunk my tea out of a Union Jack tea cup. Of course, I had read the flyers that came through the door, but I was still confused …

For instance, the Brexit flyer pointed out that if we stayed in the EU, Parliament would move to Istanbul; cars would have a maximum of three wheels; ladders would only have one rung; new-born North Sea fish would have to carry photo-ID; migrants would have first dibs on chocolate; grass would be yellow; farts would be methane-free; The Archers would become *'Les Flècheurs'* (and Home Farm's new bull would be trans); black pudding would be illegal; and every family would be £100,000 a year poorer.

The 'Remain' campaign flyer, however, while conceding these points, quite reasonably said that, after Brexit, Donald Trump would be US President; Morris dancing GCSE would replace French; coffee would taste of turnip; Lidl would only sell stuff made in Britain, (empty cardboard boxes, misshapen potatoes, and Cruise missiles); garlic would be illegal; worker bees would have to hum patriotic songs, (whilst, like the rest of us, working 18-hour days); human rights would not apply to human lefts; the English would have to holiday in Widnes; and every family would be £100,000 a year poorer.

All of this left me very unclear which way to vote.

But now, the British people have spoken, and have decided that 28 EU members will become 27. The UK goes it alone. For most of us, I expect, our decision was heavily influenced by spin. Even now, as the politicians get stuck into re-spinning the result, I am not sure that we really know where this all will lead.

What (you might reasonably be thinking) does this have to do with rural women's groups in distant Africa? Well, here is my point, admittedly arrived at by a gossamer-thin thread of rhetorical continuity: over here, we are severing links. Over there, they are forming them. Over here

Brexiting; over there ... well, I am not sure that we have a verb for it yet, but doing-together-what-we-could-not-do-apart.

Within the next few weeks, the 11 women's groups in up-country Morogoro and Tanga will be finalising their ideas for tackling maternal and child death, in a territory which has one of the worst rates for such tragedies in the peaceful world. Each hamlet will come up with its own priorities. Some of these will be specific to that community – eg growing food; sanitation systems; microloans for kick-starting cottage industry; emergency transport systems for women in labour etc. Other aspirations might be shared across several – or even all – of the hamlets; eg training of birth assistants; access to primary school; clean water etc.

Of course, it will not be like the EU: I don't envisage the women's groups becoming a common market, with trade subsidies, porridge mountains and better working conditions for goats. However, there is the idea that cooperation and synergy will become possible in a way previously inaccessible ... led by village women, whose common sense gives them common purpose.

The idea of one of the groups becoming sufficiently prosperous and self-absorbed to Brexit from the others is, as yet, only a distant contingency.

History has something to say about this cooperative approach in sub-Saharan Africa.

More than 50 years ago, Tanganyika, (as it was then), received its independence from its colonial past, (as did 28 other African nations in those heady and hopeful days of the 1960s.) Fortunately for Tanzania, despite its abject poverty, almost complete lack of infrastructure, lack of mineral resources and almost universal illiteracy, it had Julius Nyerere. 'Mwalimu', as he was affectionately known, was a teacher and chief of the Zanaki tribe. He had a vision for national unity and cooperation not seen in almost any other country. Despite there being 126 languages and even more tribes, with no sense for most people of being part of a whole, Nyerere forged a nation.

Half a century later, there has been no war or coup; everyone learns a common language (Swahili), as well as their own tribal tongue; and Muslims and Christians work and live alongside each other in every institution and every town. The country is still desperately poor, and is still mightily challenged in too many ways – but it is climbing its way out of the Iron Age with mainly a good heart. By contrast, for many of the 28 others, life is a tapestry of corruption, war, violence to women and intolerance.

The message for us, then, is to hope that Brexit does not preclude cooperation, tolerance and unity around a greater purpose than individualism. However, there is one more point to make in the parallel between *Tushikamane* and the EU. Surprisingly for me, it is not a bleeding-heart-liberal, sentimental-softie observation, but rather one which speaks to capitalism and self-interest.

A Walmart derivative has replaced your mum's corner shop. Your mate's uncle's garage is now owned by Shell. If you are younger than 30 (and some people are), you will never have browsed in an old-fashioned book shop. Your meat comes from Argentina, your flowers from Holland, your trainers from China and your bad taste in clothes from Australia. (Only joking, guys.) You can read this book on a Web that is World Wide.

We have one planet. The interests of others, are, eventually, our own interests. Global problems are our problems, and we ignore them at our peril.

As we head for Brexit, and for a firmer sense of national identity, let us hope that this will bring with it a firmer sense of mutual responsibility and cooperation for the good of all. Together, lest we forget.

Peaks and troughs

A thick white hoar-frost on the grass, the stone walls, the twigs, the lichen. Low, golden winter sun picking out the last autumnal colours of the sturdy oaks in the valley far below. A distant twisting river, fed by sparkling springs. Sheep. Pubs with good ale, good pie and good fires in inglenooks. Walking trails that are steeply uphill in both directions. Finding yourself thinking about coronary stenting and knee replacement. Blisters. More sheep. More pubs. The Peak District on a cold winter's day. Beautiful.

We were there with Mollie and Tom, (our third daughter and her husband, for those who don't know), (and for those who do), just to spend some time together and to breathe some hoary hill air.

Shatton Hall, where we stayed, originated an extraordinary seven centuries ago. (To give you a sense of scale, that was when, in China, the Ming Dynasty was just beginning to stockpile ginger; and in England, the peasants were revolting). The old house lies beneath the newer build, but even those 'new' rough yellow stones were laid before anyone had heard of America, far less wanted to be President of it; and when trumps were rude noises. The two-mile track from the village of Shatton is rutted and sunken by centuries of use. Clean water comes from a spring and, for many a long year, found its way, gratefully used, back to the same source (a little further down, and a little less potable).

England then; Tanzania now. It is salutary to think that, even in our sophisticated and highly developed England, there was a time when most of our ancestors lived in tiny hamlets; were lucky to survive childbirth; were ravaged by diseases with no access to medical care; and struggled for bare subsistence. Food needed to be grown and animals raised, or you would starve. A bad winter after a bad harvest, and the grim reaper and his pestilences would gather in the vulnerable.

Then, as now, the most vulnerable were pregnant women. In England, the peak maternal mortality rate was pre-industrial revolution, where 1% of women died when they had a baby. Given the lack of contraception, and the general-held misconception that having more children was a good insurance policy, this meant that, after five or ten children, each woman had a 5% to 10% chance of dying in childbirth.

So here is a challenge: what would you do about it? If you time-travelled back 300 years to rural England, and found this level of tragedy in pregnancy and childbirth, how would you set about tackling it? Making change is not as easy as it seems. Not only are rural mothers slow to change what they have always done, and what they have always known, but so are we – the human race.

(An example close to home is the blight of the sat-nav, to which menace my addicted wife seems oblivious. Two weeks ago for instance, she wanted to use it to get from Yorkshire to Lancashire, and the sat-nav suggested using the motorway! Huh! How wrong can you be? She wanted to follow its tyrannical advice, instead of using my map-reading skills to look for unlikely moorland sheep tracks to avoid the traffic.

I think she learnt her lesson. If we had used the sat-nav, we would never have seen the blizzard on the Snake Pass; we would never have had the excitement of being turned back from impassable roads; never have had so much time to appreciate the road works of Rochdale; never realised how out-of-the-way Halifax is; and never listened to four hours of Alan Bennett talking wryly about all the fun things he gets up to. And she still insists on using it!)

The history of tackling maternal mortality highlights this human weakness, of obstinacy in the face of reason: The main causes of mothers dying in childbirth three centuries ago were bleeding, infection and eclampsia (a type of blood pressure problem in pregnancy). The breakthrough advances were ergometrine injection for bleeding after delivery; hand-washing with antiseptics before managing childbirth; and magnesium sulphate injection for eclampsia. These were discovered respectively in 1932, 1847 and 1924. They became routinely adopted an average of 70 years later. Yes, really, 70 years. In the case of handwashing with carbolic, its instigator (Semmelweiss), who had produced a sevenfold-reduction in maternal mortality in his unit, was so ridiculed by the establishment, that years later, a broken man, he died in a mental asylum.

Here is an upbeat take on things, however, with profound relevance for *Tushikamane*: despite these stories of the mind-numbing obduracy that we humans display in accepting that we might be wrong in our assumptions, in the late 19th century, maternal mortality began to fall.

By the 20th century, it was tumbling in the USA. Between 1900 and 1990, maternal mortality dropped nearly 100-fold. In the same period, a woman's life expectancy rose from 48 to 80 years. Please note that the fall from peak levels had began before 1900. Then, in 1940, before the introduction of antibiotics, when the majority of women still delivered at home, and the world was at war, the improvement became an even stronger trend. Is it a coincidence that the fall began with the start of female emancipation? And that the 1940s were the first time in England that women were really taken seriously, occupying the responsibilities of their fighting men, and often out-performing them? Is this just feminist rant?

No, it is not feminist rant. It only takes a little thought to realise that the answer to making an impact on maternal mortality of course begins with the women themselves. In the days when women, filled with habits and traditions and myths and superstitions, were given in marriage to be baby machines and housewives, with no voice, no education and sometimes no hope, no progress could occur. For advancement of society, women had to accept the need for hygiene in childbirth; to see the need to be well-nourished in pregnancy; to be willing to accept and pay for skilled antenatal and intrapartum care; to live healthier life styles and so boost immunity to infections and avoid anaemia; to recognise the need to limit family size; and to thirst for the education which might enhance all these advances.

The profoundly dramatic changes in the health of women and their babies which has taken place in the last century and a half – in some countries at least – have been made possible by the awakening and empowerment of women.

In rural Tunguli and Msamvu, women have truly awoken. There is now an energy and a passion to climb out of the wretchedness of the situation that as many mothers and under-fives still die, as used to die in England at our pre-industrial peak.

As by now you know, this awakening is called 'Tushikamane' – 'working together, we are empowered'. In the blog page below, you can find details of the 11 women's groups and their aspirations, as observed by seasoned Tanzanian NGO workers, who recently visited and came away immensely impressed.

http://yellowchuckchucks.blogspot.co.uk/2016/12/for-reference-december-2016-state-of.html

What is beginning to emerge should have been obvious: each hamlet has different needs, different resources, different characters, different priorities. Some have too much water; some need a pump to be fixed. Some need wire for the chicken run; some need troughs for the pigs. Some want machines for sewing; some want seed for the garden.

By awakening the latent energy within each, we suddenly find that they are beginning to fix their own problems, and are beginning to be passionate about self-determination.

There has also been an unlooked-for and profound development, however. Suddenly, when women's groups have been formed, educated and given a voice, there has been an astonishing enhancement of engagement – with health, with each other and with those government agencies responsible for development. Many children have been immunised. Many more women are engaging with health services in their pregnancies. New, young, vocal female champions and leaders are beginning to find their feet.

Even more encouragingly, this awakening of engagement seems to be mutually-enhancing. Those involved in health care, who have been deeply involved in the *Tushikamane* project, are now looking beyond the walls of the clinic, and have helped the groups together to formulate the first draft of a three-year plan.

http://yellowchuckchucks.blogspot.co.uk/2016/12/first-draft-tushikamaneproject.html

This extraordinary achievement, within less than a year from taking the first steps, and less than three from the first thoughts, shows how much energy can be unleashed in rural Africa when the right steps are taken by the right people.

And so, to wrap up this first phase of development: *Tushikamane* gives young African women a voice where they never had one. That voice is now breathing life into communities whose aspirations have, until now, been subsistence and survival – and even then, not always met.

'*Tushikamane*'. Sticking together, we are empowered. Let's do it.

Nine months later ...

I had expected the chickens (and that they would cross the road). Beans, also, and bricks had been on my short-list. I even expected some pigs and some home-made school uniforms. As you will know if you reached this far in the book, we set no rules for the projects that would be born from empowering the women's groups in tiny hamlets in the Tanzanian bush. Their mission, as you remember, was to reduce the appalling rates of maternal and child mortality by boosting nutrition, reducing abject poverty and enhancing any aspect of community health and development which might possibly serve the purpose.

So, yes, I had expected that some families might find themselves with an extra bit of protein or an extra few shillings with which to part-pay the costs of illness or of childbirth or of sending girls to school. Maybe some would even begin on the vital but daunting project of improving water and sanitation.

What I had not expected – not at all, not one bit – was that they would simply just stop the awfulness of female genital mutilation. Or that those communities, who, for generations had steadfastly resisted new-fangled health interventions, despite a 10% child mortality rate, would suddenly start getting their children immunised. Or that women in labour – sometimes even accompanied by their traditional birth attendants – would start seeking help in difficulty, before it was too late. Or that some of these TBAs would themselves be asking for training. Or that this year, in these remote and under-developed hamlets, the grim reaper has yet to claim its most gruesome and tragic victim – a maternal death.

What has happened? What is this amazing firework lighting up the Tanzanian sky? Not exactly what we thought anyway, when we lit the fuse. I have been giving this much thought, and a number of allegorical explanations have occurred to me. Given that as I write this, it is the quincentenary of his 95 theses being nailed to a door in Wittenberg, I think I am going to muse on the protest of Martin Luther – someone who also was part of a world in which an ancient set of rules and traditions were being turned upside down.

(Whatever your religious persuasion, by the way, and however seismic the consequences of his protest, one has to question the sensitivity of nailing stuff to a door as a means of communication. What if neighbours started doing it?)

> "Bang Bang Bang. Thanks for the sugar. Here's your cup back. Bang. Sorry it's a bit cracked."

Or Parcel Force?:
> "Bang Bang Bang. Sorry we missed you. Bang. Here's your parcel."

Or even technophobes who eschew electronic messaging in favour of real paper?:
> "Bang Bang Bang. Thanks for the text. Yes, 7 o'clock would be fine.")

Anyway, 453 years before the invention of Blu Tack, that is how the Rev Dr Luther chose to deliver his challenge to the might of Rome. My point, however, is this: why did this man's bold and uncompromising challenge re-write European history, and foment the most profound societal reform in a thousand or more years? Surely many others had been also harbouring similar thoughts? Indeed, they must have been, for Protestantism to have developed so swiftly. So why had there not just been a gradual trickle of influence, building slowly to a river and then a flood of rebelliousness against buying your way into heaven? All done slowly enough to let people come to terms with the new, and gradually to let go of any bad in the old?

Instead, one moment it seems that every priest in Europe is a papist; and the next, papists are hiding from hideous recriminations, in a hidden chamber between the drawing room hearth and the scullery, planning a moonlight flit via a secret passage under the quince tree to the kitchen garden.

The origins and explanations of this, one of history's more important conflagrations, are complex and many-faceted. However, I would like to pick up just a few smouldering thoughts, with which to shine a light on *Tushikamane's* new and wonderful African mini-reformation. For in Tanzania there must also have been generations of would-be dissidents, who would have quite liked to have nailed a women-and-children's-charter to a tree, but didn't. Women who would have quite liked to avoid FGM; who would have quite liked their children to have been immunised; who would have quite liked to have got to hospital in childbirth before it was too late. But didn't.

The first point that occurs to me is this self-evident one: the more rigid the straitjacket within which a culture is nurtured, the less able are the individuals to rebel, even in a trickle of dissidence, far less a flood. But here is an irony: when a traditional hierarchy aspires to be benevolent, perhaps it becomes even harder for the lowly to challenge the leaders on their follies. It would seem churlish to have a go at a leadership trying to do its best for you, especially when they are doing so with an unwavering commitment to tradition and status.

Leadership follies thus blossom into peccadilloes, and peccadilloes become armadillos. (Not my best metaphor, but it sort-of wrote itself, and anyway, you get the point.) Meanwhile, the people continue to do what they have always done, not because it is always a good idea, but because it is always what they have done. From the hierarchy's point of view, you cannot pick and choose which tradition you like, which decision you like, and which you do not. You inherit the entire lot – the culture, the traditions and the paternalism – and you pass it on.

A passivity thereby grows up, particularly among the vulnerable – which, in almost every culture on earth, have traditionally been the young women and their babies. Female Genital Mutilation. Childhood death. Have six children. No female education. Fetch the water, fetch the firewood, cook, clean, die. Best not think too much about it all. Count your blessings.

No-one in a benevolent autocracy – not the leaders, not the men of the village and least of all the women themselves – intend that bad things should come with the good. But there is no space in the cultural evolution for careful discernment and planned change. No platform for the voices of disagreement. When poorly-educated, rural traditional societies in resource-poor cultures are trying to be benevolent, there is therefore a built-in latency which implicitly and steadfastly opposes change. As with Luther (and presumably millions of his contemporaries), perhaps people in such cultures tend just to put up with things that they do not agree with … perhaps doing so for far too long, until a valve blows in the society's engine and the steam rushes out.

Before I go on, I think I ought to challenge what seems to be the assumption behind these thoughts that, by and large, it is men who are the dominators, and women the dominated. Is the desire to dominate archetypally a male trait? Kobudai fish say "yes", while Hilary Clinton, Maggie Thatcher and Boudicca say "no". (And of course Queen Khaleesi of Game of Thrones, who maybe even invented 'no'.)

Let's take the 'ayes' first: Up to middle age, Kobudai fish, amazingly, are all female, (as exquisitely illustrated in Blue Planet 2). Life is all fish chat, sardine mornings and making krill jam in autumn. (If my wife is reading this: only joking, darling.) Genuinely, however, these extra-ordinary marine enigmas manifest as shoals of younger females, prowled on the periphery by big fat ugly old males … who dominate each other, and the females. (Any resemblance to the Houses of Parliament is strictly coincidental.) When one or two dominant males move on, something happens to the biggest females. They sullenly shuffle off to a cave. They eat lots, and swill down more sea-water than is good for them. They lose their social skills. They brood on life. These activities seem to switch off the female hormones, and switch on the male ones. A month or two later, they emerge … as males.

The first thing they do is to seek out any smaller male, and give him a bit of a finning. Then they eat a bit more, and then get on with the business of procreating the next generation of daughters.

The inescapable conclusion (for Kobudai, anyway) is that the male hormone and the desire to dominate seem to go hand-in-hand. Bulls, lions, rutting stags and a host of Father Nature's other mammals and birds seem to agree.

Hilary, Maggie and Boudicca would point out, however, that it does not have to be thus. Traditionally male-dominated societies and cultures seem to have the capacity for encompassing the voice of women – under certain circumstances. In the UK, universal suffrage for women came in 1928. It our case, the final push had been provided by the First World War, where women successfully took on male roles.

(By the way, it is a little-appreciated fact that it was in the same Act of Parliament that all men acquired the right to vote. Prior to World War One, only 40% of men were eligible, with the most vulnerable men excluded, in a society where status was one of the most important operators:

> "Alright Guv'ner, har's it goin'?! Me and the missus want ter say 'appy Christmas to you an' all at the Manor, and 'er indoors sends this bot'l o' potted turnip fer yer Christmas vittles!
>
> "Thanks awfully, my man. Take it round to the servants' entrance, and the second footman will deal with it. Then come back and clean up those boot-prints on the step.")

So, finally, in the UK in 1928, a big fat nail was driven into what one day will be the coffin of all-pervasive upper-class male dominance. What women received that year was legitimacy. A platform. A voice. From there, it has been possible steadily to unpick the uglier parts of our culture's tapestry and to weave in some bright new threads. We now, for the most part, provide for and protect the disadvantaged and the needy. No priest-holes were necessary. No Inquisition. Nothing nailed to a door. The natural respect for women that was already represented in the enlightened, found legitimate expression, and led to progress.

In Tanzania, many rural villagers for generations have been performing FGM, avoiding immunisation and eschewing modern health interventions. Suddenly now, in Tunguli and Msamvu, it is different. I wonder, then, whether an undercurrent of rebellion – by both men and women – against the inadequacies of tradition has suddenly found a channel in *Tushikamane*. Not just an outlet, but a legitimate outlet, and so we now find the unsavoury beginning to be steam-cleaned away.

Is it too much to hope that this will be an irrevocable advance? An advance that, generation after generation, will close the 100-fold gap between their mortality rates and ours?

Well, I will be dead before we know the answer. But if you are reading this in 2060, and wonderful things have happened with emancipation of women in rural Africa, no need to shout it from the rooftops.

Just nail it to a nearby door.

Post Script

Since this was written, further visitors from 'Mission Morogoro', (the host charity of Tushikamane), have been to Tunguli and Msamvu.

Wonderful things are happening.

Mission Morogoro, (whose members pay every penny of any expenses from their own pockets), have for many years been delivering development projects in Tunguli, but each one self-contained, and with innumerable threats to sustainability.

Now that they have not just community buy-in, but positive self-starting and commitment, a new and exciting progress is taking place. Hamlets that have never had clean water in their history, now have wells that they know how to maintain. Sewing projects have sewing machines. Fields for ploughing have a tractor. Subsistence farmers have seed. Hungry families have chickens.

An important and evolving part of this story needs important emphasis: It is this: Where in the past things were 'done' to hamlets, with the best of intentions, now there exists a three-sided concord:

1. the women's groups providing impetus, prioritisation, energy and labour, as well as getting right down and working hard;
2. Mission Morogoro, providing, amongst other things, money, materials, wisdom and support;
3. And finally, as we are beginning to discover, a third element really adds a magical sprinkling of sustainability: working with highly professional non-for-profit Tanzanian ('NPO') partners, who really know what needs doing, and how to do it: Tanzanian NPOs with professionals in key fields: water & sanitation; appropriate technology; microfinance; agriculture; etc etc. For each of these, there exist wonderful, focused, mobile, effective organisations, peopled by caring and charismatic professionals.

Each new project is a step towards the twenty-first century.

For an example, we might look at the remote hamlet of Kwibomba. Like all the other Tushikamane groups, the women of Kwibomba highlighted the need for accessible clean water. They, and their daughters, walked many mile, five times a day, to access this:

Cue 'SAWA' – Sanitation and Water Action – http://sawatanzania.org/

SAWA are an NPO whose wonderful staff first undertook a detailed survey of need. They then mobilised and educated the appropriate people of the hamlet, not only in how to build and maintain a good well, but also in issues such as prevention of water-borne infection:

The men and women of the hamlet then provided labour; SAWA provided expertise; and Mission Morogoro provided just £500, to result in this:

The difference to the hamlet, and to the lives of the women and girls, is incalculable.

Tushikamane! Let's do it together!

For progress reports and uplifting stories on Tushikamane, please go to: http://www.missionmorogoro.org.uk/

and

http://yellowchuckchucks.blogspot.co.uk

29418475R00102

Printed in Great Britain
by Amazon